Understanding Addiction:

Propensity, Progression, Crisis and Recovery

Christopher J. O'Brien, M. S.

Copyright © 2012 by Christopher J. O'Brien.

All rights reserved.

Except as permitted under the United States Copyright Act of 1976, no part of this publication may be reproduced or distributed in any form or by any means, or stored in a database or retrieval system, without prior written permission of the publisher.

Published in the United States by:
Medallion Publishing Company, Inc.
P. O. Box 14336
North Palm Beach, FL 33408
www.medallionpublishing.com

Written By: O'Brien, Christopher J., 1947–
Understanding Addiction: Propensity, Progression, Crisis & Recovery
Edited by: Kaiulani Winter
Cover Design and Typesetting by: Patricia Rasch
Printed in the U.S.A. by 360 Digital Books.

ISBN-10: 0985796405
ISBN-13: 978-0-9857964-0-2

Library of Congress Control Number 2012917583

Limit of Liability/Disclaimer of Warranty: While the author has used their best efforts in preparing this book, they make no representations or warranties with respect to the accuracy or completeness of the contents of this book and specifically disclaim any implied warranties of merchantability or fitness for a particular purpose. Neither the publisher nor author shall be liable for any damages, including but not limited to special, incidental, consequential or other damages.

10 9 8 7 6 5 4 3

Contents

Context 1
Established Concepts and Perspectives. 5
Components of Addiction—Bio psychosocial. 11
Self-Esteem—The Biology of Conscience 17
    The Biology of Conscience (short form) 17
    The Biology of Conscience (long form) 19
Feelings 27
Propensity for Addiction 33
    Propensity for Addiction—Biological 34
    Propensity for Addiction—Psychological 36
    Propensity for Addiction—Sociocultural 41
Progression. 45
    Progression—Biological 45
    Progression—Psychological 46
    Progression—Socio-cultural. 49
    Progression—Spiritual/Moral 52
Addiction—Crisis. 55
    Crisis—Obstruction 55
    Crisis—Importance 56
    Crisis—Biological. 57
    Crisis—Psychological. 59
    Crisis—Socio/Cultural. 60
    Crisis—Spiritual/Moral 62
Addiction—Recovery. 65
    Definition. 65
    Recovery—Biological. 66
    Recovery—Psychological. 67
    Recovery—Socio-Cultural. 69
    Recovery—Spiritual/Moral 71
References 77

Context

Who We Serve

This work, while apparently academic and clinical, is, nevertheless, a human effort to reduce suffering. I am profoundly motivated by the memory of those who we were unable to reach. I am haunted by the charming and sweet woman barely 30 years old who, upon abstaining from alcohol, lapsed into an eating disorder which alienated her from society until she took her life by a bullet to the temple. She chose this apparently inexplicable path in spite of superhuman efforts by her friends, family, and mental health professionals. I recall the man who we found on the street, destitute, dirty who, upon achieving sobriety was discovered to be a retired school teacher whose life had been dedicated to teaching the most difficult inner city children. Though physically ravaged by years of alcohol abuse, he rededicated himself to serving recovering persons. There was the attractive young woman who could not stop prostituting herself to fuel her drug habit. Early recovery and therapy discovered that, at the age of 4, her grandmother held her down while her grandfather had intercourse with her.

For You

You might be struggling with your own addiction. You might feel powerless over the addiction of a person who is close to you. You might be a dedicated member of the helping professions. Regardless of who you are, we sincerely hope that this work serves you well.

Social Context

In 2010, 48.2% of students in grade 12 had used some mood and mind-altering substance at some time. (Johnston, O'Malley, Bachman, & Schulenberg, 2010, table 5.1). While this statistic might seem alarming to some, others might comment that this number is surprisingly low. Popular notions might exaggerate and exclaim that "… it seems that everybody is high on one drug or another…" Regardless of the numbers, addiction is one of the most challenging social and health issues of our time.

History

Inaba & Cohen (2007) is one of the most cited, comprehensive, and recent texts on addiction. They offer several points which accentuate the importance of understanding addiction:

> "The history of man reflects the integral part that psychoactive drugs have played in the social, economic, and emotional development of civilizations; and through the current drug of choice often changes, the reasons for drug use remain the same." (p. 2).

Addiction is not just a modern phenomenon.

Addiction, Crime & Violence

As we discuss addiction, we note the relationship between addiction and crime. DOHHS (1990) examines the relationship between drugs and violence. Notably, "… analysis of data from a series of studies on family violence… suggest(s) that alcohol abuse is a greater risk factor than is illicit drug use" (p. 15). While popular perceptions support the relationship between substance abuse and crime, specific information about the strong relationship between the two is offered at a website created by the U. S. Bureau of Justice Statistics (BJS, 2011). Notably, there are those who committed crimes to pay for drugs and alcohol, as well as those who were under the influence at the time of their offense. This is not to belabor the point, but to support the idea that addiction, while a profound personal and family problem, is also a pervasive social problem.

Addiction as a Pervasive Social Issue

Therefore, I suggest that the case of addiction cannot be separated from culture, technology, or politics. For example, crime is not caused by substance abuse, nor is substance abuse caused by criminals or criminal behavior. I suggest that there is a complex relationship between crime and substance abuse which is also related to the change in the traditional family structure. But these cannot be separated from the free market society, the conquering of certain diseases, infant mortality rates, and human rights.

Summary

Addiction and its relationship to our society as a whole is a complex social dilemma. Likewise, addiction is external evidence of the internal dilemmas and complexities of the human experience. This work will strive to examine and describe the nature of addiction by beginning with a description of the human experience itself. I propose to offer an illustration of addiction pathology sufficient that the employer, the family member, the spouse, the friend, the parent, the addiction professional, and the addict himself or herself will react to these perspectives with an internal "aha". This perspective, it is hoped, will replace the previous exclamations like: Why don't you just stop? Why can't I stop? But you would stop, if you loved me. Why would you want to hurt yourself? Haven't you had enough? Please stop! Why do I feel worse when I eat? Why do I eat when I'm sad? Why do I cut myself? Why would you want to cut yourself?

Personal Challenges

As the previous writing moved from the clinical to the personal perspective, I note that one of the greatest challenges of the mental health care and the addiction professional is the profound emotional strain of watching people who, in spite of being intelligent and apparently capable, continue to destroy themselves before our eyes. This is in spite of superhuman efforts at studies and interventions by incredibly talented and caring friends, family members and professionals.

These few examples illustrate the profound importance of improving the manner in which we serve these people: our families, friends, and patients. It is to this purpose that I dedicate this work.

Our Mission

So, our mission here is to draw on the experience and expertise of these incredibly talented and dedicated people who have gone before us. We hope to bring together their knowledge and experience to construct a new understanding of the nature of addiction. With this new paradigm, we hope to foster a deeper understanding and simplification of the complexities of addiction which, in our perception, reflect the complexities of the human condition.

Established Concepts and Perspectives

Before we begin the description of addiction, it is important to note that our descriptions conform to accepted concepts, for the most part. While it is suggested that this work will offer new and deeper perspectives on addiction, it is important to reaffirm that it does not contradict established concepts. Rather, it attempts to first reaffirm the core concepts of human personality and then build upon them. Throughout this work, we will seek to base our observations and conclusions upon accepted scholarly and academic sources. While we might expand upon or extend the work of others, it is observed that addiction professionals are committed to applying only those interventions which are adequately supported. Above all, it is our mission to do no harm.

Definitions

We shall define addiction as: "The human condition in which the individual has lost the capacity for self-determination". The power of self-determination might be observed as a general synonym for "ability to function productively" or "ability to cope". Further dialogues on the topic might include a discussion of "resiliency", mental health, physical health or any other aspect of a person who is coping adequately, retains the power of self-determination, and seems to be able to make choices which are consistent with "self-actualization" (Maslow, 1943, Rogers,

1961). In contrast, a popular observation about addiction is that the person who presents as "addicted" is making decisions which are self-destructive. This is the dilemma and apparent insanity of addiction. The term "self-actualization" as used here is generally as described by Maslow (1943) and Rogers (1961), although the concept will be expanded upon in later discussions.

Terminology—Disease

An aside at this juncture might be a discussion of the terminology we use. There is an intentional avoidance of the word "disease" to describe addiction. The disease concept or definition of alcoholism is a political or cultural concept which is used for the allocation of health care resources, including welfare and health insurance. The "disease" terminology implies a number of connotations about addiction. This is not to discount the disease concept. This is, however, an effort to encourage the reader to maintain an open mind. It will be argued that addiction is a condition of the whole person; much more than a disease. Later, it might be observed that, under some circumstances, addiction is a disease. But in other cases, it might not be seen as a disease. That is, some addictions might be clinically observed to contain the necessary components to qualify as a disease, but some might not.

Of particular interest is the experience where mood and mind altering substances and behaviors might be viewed as valid, though extreme, coping mechanisms. There has been more than one recovering person who has stood at a lectern and affirmed "Thank God for alcohol" to describe the incredibly painful life experience which the substance effectively anesthetized until the person was able or ready to face it. For example, a 14 year old girl was grateful for alcohol when her mother died and her father abandoned her. She used alcohol to survive until she became old enough to stop, and look back to experience her grief. She expressed how, when she became and adult she was finally able to attempt sobriety. Through the peer support in a 12-step fellowship and the added assistance of clinical psychotherapy, she faced her loss, experienced valid grief, and began to rebuild her sense of self in order to cope with life.

In this case, the life experience of this woman displayed a "dependency" upon alcohol as clinically defined. However, it is not difficult to argue that alcohol dependency might have been her best avenue to survive and finally prosper in light of the life challenges which she encountered.

Terminology—Insanity

Another important term is the word "insanity". Clinically, we speak of disorders. The word insanity has some emotional value in that it is an exclamation or a pejorative which is applied to behavior or thoughts that make no logical sense. In this description of addiction, we will present the idea that addiction might be seen as a disorder. Likewise, the behavior might be described as "insane" because it makes no sense for someone to behave in a manner which is harmful. However, it will be an important aspect of our understanding here to assert the idea that addictive behavior is insane, but it makes perfect sense when we understand the structure of addiction. That is, behavior which seems "insane" or makes no sense in the present might make perfect sense when viewed in the context of the past.

Clear Explanation

Our goal here might be to demonstrate that addiction need not be a great mystery. If we consider the idea that addictive behavior can be clearly explained and understood, the behavior will no longer be so puzzling. In the case of addiction, behavior which might appear illogical or insane in the present might make perfect sense when we observe the personal history of the addicted person. The behavioral pathways and construct of human personality which manifest addiction can be observed and understood. Addiction might not be viewed either as a disease or a form of insanity. Addiction is a human condition which is a product of all the factors which define the human condition itself.

Cross Addiction

The American Medical Association's published position on alcoholism emphasizes the correlation between alcohol and cigarette addiction. One can find freedom from alcohol dependence and discover that they are left with an addiction to nicotine, overeating, gambling, marijuana, or prescription medication. Addiction substances and habits appear to be interchangeable. This idea that addictions can be interchangeable argues that there is, sometimes, something other than the substance itself which plays a part in the pathology of addiction.

Addictive Behaviors

Inaba & Cohen (2007) also assert that "Compulsive behaviors, such as binge-eating, anorexia, bulimia, compulsive gambling, sexual compulsion, Internet addiction, compulsive shopping, and even codependency, affect many of the same areas of the brain that are influenced by psychoactive drugs." (p. 2). This connection between substance abuse and compulsive behaviors is reasonably widely accepted today. Many educational venues caption courses as some combination of "Substance Abuse and Addictive Behaviors".

Holistic Perspective

Throughout this discussion one might observe the underlying idea that the understanding of addiction is directly related to understanding the human condition. This concept will lead to the idea that to understand addiction requires an understanding of the individual who is addicted. The phenomenological condition of addiction can only be understood if one understands the whole person; the individual who suffers from the condition. Baler, & Volkow, (2011) is offered to support this viewpoint:

> "The view of drug addiction as a systems failure should help refocus our general approach to developing dynamic models and early comprehensive interventions that optimize the ways in which we prevent and treat a complex, developmental disorder such as drug addiction." (Abstract)

Based upon my experience, I suggest that, if we can understand the person, we can understand the addiction. This is with the hope that, with greater understanding, we can assist the addicted person to regain the power of self determination.

The Human Condition

We will begin by examining the human condition in a context which is widely accepted by academia and popular sources. Referring back to a widely accepted discussion on the human function, we reference Abraham Maslow's (1943) hierarchy of human needs.

As we suggest here that addiction is a condition of the whole person, Maslow (1943) writes: "The integrated wholeness of the organism must be one of the foundation stones of motivation theory" (location 4-15). Maslow (1945) identifies first the *physiological* needs. The capacity for self-determination (the ability to function) requires physical resources of physical sustenance (i. e., food and water). Next in order of importance are the *safety* needs. Maslow's (1943) discussion here speaks to the desire for order, and routine and the need to perceive that those with whom we associate are not aggressive or dangerous to us. Next Maslow (1943) suggests that there are *love* needs. Finally, Maslow (1943) observes the human need for *self-actualization*.

Later in his discussions, Maslow (1943) identifies the *desire to know and understand*.

As one observes Maslow's dialogue one might see an effort to more clearly describe the human condition with definitions of needs and their interrelationships. In short order, the manner in which these needs come together becomes so intertwined that it defies quantitative analysis. It defies logic. In our context, it is suggested that the most useful term to describe the human experience is liberally applied by Carl Rogers (1961). Rogers refers to the human experience as "phenomenological". This point is important here as a core concept in addiction understanding and treatment. We must observe and serve each person with recognition of their unique phenomenological circumstance.

As Maslow (1943) discusses the hierarchy of these needs and suggests that the physiological needs precede the safety and love needs, we are reminded of the experiments by Harry Harlow (Harlow, Dodsworth, & Harlow, 1965). Harlow separated young Rhesus monkeys from their mothers and demonstrated that, sometimes, love and affection can be more important than food.

Further observations demonstrated the limited ability to cope which is the result of early parental abandonment in Rhesus monkeys. The young monkeys who were separated from their mothers were observed to be incapable of functioning in monkey society. This inability to cope was a permanent disability, in some cases. In some cases, the monkeys who were separated from their mothers died, even though they were provided with food and water. Harlow, Dodsworth, & Harlow (1965) described this fatality thus:

> "One of six monkeys isolated for 3 months refused to eat after release and died 5 days later. The autopsy report attributed death to emotional anorexia. (p. 92)"

We offer this study to illustrate the profound limitation in the ability to function which might be caused by early childhood trauma or parental abandonment. With this observation in mind, we accept the list of human needs as offered by Maslow (1943) but observe that the developmental and affectionate needs of human beings can transcend food, water, and shelter. As we observe addiction, we note that the emotional pain of social isolation can be more severe than physical pain, or hunger. These experiments illustrate the profound impact of emotional pain for human beings, and reduce some of the apparent mystery of addiction. This relationship between emotional pain and addiction will be central to our later discussions.

Component Perspectives

Having described the profound complexity of the human personality and addiction pathology, it is hoped that the reader now yearns for a model of addiction which enables us to separate the components of addiction in an effort to wrap our logical minds about it. Only by breaking it down into its components can we begin to observe the pathology of addiction. If we can break it down and digest it in pieces, perhaps we can come to a greater understanding.

Summary

We will describe the human experience using widely accepted concepts. We acknowledge the complexity and holistic characteristics of the human experience and addiction. We accept the idea that mood altering substances are not evil in themselves, and that pharmacological science has the capacity to reduce suffering and benefit humanity.

Components of Addiction— Bio psychosocial

The Phenomenological Human Experience

Rogers (1961), one of the most widely read and admired mental health professionals of our time, describes the human experience as "phenomenological". As previously stated, it is our impression that the nature of addiction reflects the nature of the human experience itself. Therefore we have adapted and adopted this term: "phenomenological" to express the complex and multi-faceted aspects of human behavior and addiction.

But we will expand the definition of the word. What is important here is the idea that the human experience and the construct of human personality are not based entirely on cognitive concepts. That is, conversation and awareness are important to change in human personal growth, identity, and self-actualization. But cognition is not enough. The construct of human personality is a phenomenological experience. For example, a profound childhood experience is one which captures all of the senses. Sight, smell, sound, touch, and taste. Examples of these profound experiences are childbirth, nursing (for both parties), sexual experiences, and life threatening experiences.

Grass Roots Recovery

We will expound upon these later, but we offer a prologue to that discussion as a reference to the idea that while cognitive therapies are relevant and helpful, they might be insufficient. Cognitive therapies are productive, but are most successful when accompanied by modifications in behavior and phenomenological human experiences. These experiences must be powerful enough to alter the self-destructive perceptions which were created by the phenomenological experiences of childhood or the addiction environment. On some level, this explains the apparent utility of "Grass Roots" recovery venues (AA, NA, CA, ACOA, and Al-Anon). Clinical interventions serve an essential purpose, but the phenomenological experience of life in addiction seems to require a phenomenological experience of recovery as offered in Grass Roots cultures.

The Bio psychosocial (Spiritual) Viewpoint

This allusion to the propensity for addiction in childhood trauma, the valid application of alcohol in a manner which would be clinically classified as "dependence", and the process of recovery will be integrated in our component description of this process. The reader might observe that the addiction of the young woman who lost her mother contains a psychological element. She used alcohol to medicate her intense sorrow and feeling of abandonment. This alludes to our description of the components of addiction.

In an effort to gain wider acceptance of our concepts here, we will adapt our description of the "Components Theory" of addiction to include some widely accepted clinical terminology. Addiction professionals recognize the complex nature of addiction and its profound effect on the whole person by adopting a concept known as the "Bio psychosocial Assessment". To this we will add a suggestion offered by some of my colleagues in addiction recovery with the term "Spiritual". However, our discussion and description here will bring some new perspectives on the spiritual. In 12 step fellowships, there is often the discussion of the distinction between "spiritual" and "religious". These dialogues have been observed to be heated and energetic. Our discussions here will offer new perspectives on faith, spirituality and religion. In anticipation of these new concepts, we will modestly modify the "Bio psychosocial". Notably, we will not amend it to "Biopsychosocialspiritual". Our term, and our components in component theory, will be reflected in the term "Biopsychosocialmoral". For the helping professional, the "moral" terminology is intended to refer to the moral development of a person as defined by Kohlberg, a summary of which is offered by Kohlberg & Hersh (1977). We will adapt Kohlberg's concepts to our description of addiction in an effort to acknowledge and cultivate a relationship with and the support of accepted academic and clinical concepts.

Biological—There are biological factors which influence the propensity for addiction. Some of these biological components are congenital. Some people have a naturally occurring physical response to alcohol where the euphoria which they experience at the first drink is a powerful as heroin is to others (Asbury & Ketcham, 2000). Some of the biological propensities are alterations in physiology or brain chemistry which is caused by excessive use of alcohol. Therefore, there are pre-existing and developmental aspects of the physical propensity to addiction.

Psychological—There are psychological aspects of the disease. On one front, there might be a mental disorder which persuades the individual to medicate with alcohol, drugs, or behaviors. There are developmental events which increase the emotional discomfort or decrease the ability for the individual to cope. Among these are: childhood trauma, early death of a parent, parental abandonment, or sexual abuse. In these cases, addiction might be a method of coping, or a manifestation of self-destructive behaviors based in low self-image. This concept is more recent in the study of some behaviors. We suggest that the reader refer to the works of Tuppet Yates (2009).

Social—It is interesting to note that the family circumstance might be seen as a social influence. There are families in which substance use might be judged as excessive. In these cases, the propensity for addiction might be increased by the social pressure. In the U. S. the wide acceptance of the social use of alcohol is an influence upon the propensity for addiction. It might be noteworthy that the dividing line between psychological and social might not be clearly defined.

Spiritual/Moral—The inclusion of this aspect of addiction appears to be prompted primarily by the emphasis, in grass roots recovery, of the "God" factor. There is, however, a clear relationship between guilt for acts committed and personal shortcomings as a result of addiction. Getting clean and/or sober is accompanied by the grim realization of the acts or shortcomings committed in the process which are outside of one's own moral code and conscience. The guilt associated with these acts is an emotional component which increases the propensity for relapse. Notably, this guilt might be seen as a psychological issue. This emphasizes that, while we identify the components of addiction, we cannot lose sight of how they are all inextricably interconnected.

God, Religion, Spirituality, and Morality

We anticipate that our greatest contribution to addiction theory might be this aspect of our component theory. I have heard clinicians puzzle over the "God" thing from grass roots fellowships. In this discussion, we will not threaten anyone's religion or spiritual beliefs. We will, however, bring together religion, spirituality, and the mental health professions when we demonstrate the connection between spiritual beliefs, human personality, and psychology. We believe that this synergism will be of substantial importance when understanding addiction pathology and recovery. We propose to remove much of the mysticism surrounding religion and demonstrate the nature of its benefit for mental health. This will enable the mental health professional to better assist their clients in finding their own spiritual and moral path.

Stages of Addiction

Having defined the components of addiction, we will then divide the discussion into the stages of addiction. Addiction could be defined as a process, or a system with feedback which influences the progression or the recovery from addiction. It is interesting to note that the concept of "recovery" rather than "cure" is a subject of great discussion. We choose to examine the process of addiction by defining the following stages.

Propensity For Addiction—It is important to understand that the existence of the condition is not entirely a result of present circumstance. In addition, the understanding that it has developed over a period of time has implications for blaming, morality, difficulty of intervention, and the long process of recovery.

Progression of Addiction—It is important to observe that addiction is progressive in an effort to distinguish when is a person getting worse or progressing, or when they are on the path to recovery. The understanding of progression also argues against complacency. Some might think that a "little addiction" is OK. While that might be accurate in some cases, the reality of the progression to death or destruction is an important aspect of our understanding and treatment of addiction.

Crisis and Intervention—Crisis, or what might be termed, "The tipping point" is important to understand and describe. With frustration, the grass roots recovery community often says, of an alcoholic, "He's not ready". Understanding when and why one becomes ready is an essential aspect of addiction recovery.

Recovery—Recovery as a concept recognizes that, as the "Big Book" (AA,2011, whose text is substantially unchanged since its first publication in 1939) reads, "Our liquor was but a symptom" (p.64). This, and the writing surrounding the observation describe the long term action which they define as "recovery". While the reader might not accept the ideas that addiction requires a lifetime of maintenance, there are a number of arguments which suggest the advisability of a long term program to maintain the "capacity for self-determination". While one might argue that they are "recovered", it is easy to see that, recovered or not, a lifetime of personal growth and loving service to others might be beneficial to anyone. Perhaps it is addiction which is the only force powerful enough to persuade some people to stop and engage in self-reflection.

Summary

We have defined the components and stages of addiction which will be the format of the discussion which follows. We anticipate that these classifications and terminology will assist the reader in coming to some understanding of this complex issue.

Self-Esteem— The Biology of Conscience

The Biology of Conscience (short form)

In both clinical and grass roots recovery venues, there is the continuing dilemma where we observe that the addict, whether using alcohol, drugs, gambling, anorexia, or cutting, continues self-destructive behavior in spite of all the cognitive and logical arguments to the contrary. In grass roots, the cultural myth is "…he (she) is not ready…". This is, culturally, justified by the idea "… he (she) has not suffered enough…". In clinical settings, we observe this apparent refusal to complete simple acts which, at their own admission, will save their lives. Even in a clinical setting, the client is referred to grass roots recovery to get a sponsor in an effort to cultivate the spiritual experience which, mythically and mysteriously is the salvation of the alcoholic or addict. For example: "… -once a psychic change has occurred…" (Silkworth, as cited by AA, 2001, p. xxix). Notably, the same volume refers to the process as a "spiritual experience" (AA, 2001, p.568).

Descriptions of this spiritual experience tend to preserve its mysticism. Perhaps the inability to clearly describe this process adds some level of confidence that it will work. However, we propose to more clearly identify the process in a biological and psychological context. We hope that this more pragmatic description of spirituality, God consciousness, and the psychic change will increase our ability to help others to achieve recovery. It is important to note, however, that this understanding of the concept will not, for one moment, argue for or against one's religion. On the contrary, by describing the biology of morality, conscience, and self-esteem, we propose to create some level of consistency and harmony between the behavioral sciences and the spiritual search for meaning in life.

First, we will offer the short form of our description. This will be followed with a longer form of description and argument for those who are resistant to the idea, and those who are intrigued by the idea and want more information.

We begin with the widely accepted idea of conscience. Within each person is a moral code or conscience. While this conscience might differ from one culture to another, few would argue that, with the exception of a few individuals, there is a conscience or moral code which exercises some influence over behavior. We might argue that this conscience is an essential element of self-esteem. The conscience, as an element of self-esteem, compares the behavior of the individual to the internal moral code. This is not a conscious operation. It appears to operate inexorably. Apparently, it is like a scale which measures the actions of the individual, compares these actions to the internal moral code, and returns a sense of self which then judges and values the individual. From that point, the individual tends to manifest in their life, that which is appropriate to their self-worth.

This explains the acts which seem irresistible and cause harm to the individual. It is interesting to note that this moral code is, partially, cultural. Therefore, a sense of low self-worth can be imposed by unreasonable expectations set upon the individual by a harsh environment. A well-meaning father might think that being harsh with his son will make him stronger. If, however, his expectations are above the abilities of his son, the results can be harmful. The self-perception of low worth to his family can create a behavioral tendency for self harm.

This propensity to measure one's self worth is biologically based in a process which has been termed "genetic psychology" (Wright, 1994; Sagan & Druyan, 1992). The value of the individual to his gene pool (family) can cause self-sacrifice, self-injury, or self-destruction for the benefit of the family.

Examples of this phenomenon are the willingness of the soldier to give his life for his platoon, the early death of a parent in a famine, as the food is first given to the children, and the custom among some Native American families where the elderly accept the end of life and wander into the wilderness to leave resources for their family.

Therefore, the spiritual experience is one in which some act or cognitive argument causes a profound shift in this biological conscience where the individual is liberated from the propensity for self-destruction. For some, it is a moment of clarity in which the idea of a loving Creator and a prescribed code of behavior brings a perception of self-worth and self-efficacy. In other cases, the shift is gradual, as the individual goes through the cognitive process of a personal inventory and then embarks on a process of amends. These amends, through action, begin to increase the sense of self-worth as one adopts a code of conduct in accordance with their own internal morality.

It is important to remind the reader here that, while cognitive therapies can cause a shift in perspective, and identify a new behavioral path, cognition is only part of the shift. The most effective means of influencing self-worth is personal action. Cognitive affirmations of self-worth in the absence of behavioral modification might be termed "denial". Looking in the mirror and making positive affirmations when behavior has not changed might have little effect. The phenomenological act of being of service to others has the power to manifest an undeniable perception of personal worth as a human being.

The Biology of Conscience (long form)

Essential to our understanding of some aspects of addiction is our definition of self-esteem. We suggest that self-esteem, self-concept, or the construct of human personality are inseparable. We first offer our comprehensive definition. Subsequently, we support this definition academically and scientifically.

Addiction and Self-Destruction

Throughout discussion of human behavior is the concept of self-esteem. In a previous work which is unpublished at this writing, I offered a description of self-esteem which conforms to current psychological theory, but offers some new perspectives which, in my estimation, offer some revolutionary, interesting and valuable perspectives. I offer an abridged version of that discussion to establish a tool for understanding the nature of addiction. Specifically, it is the intent of this discussion on self-esteem to provide a clear, relevant, and solid explanation of why a human being would actively seek and engage in behavior which, to others, is clearly self-destructive.

Accepted Principles

This perspective on what we call self-esteem, is a bit "out of the box." It is suggested here that this perspective on self-esteem is the most valuable idea which will be offered here. However, this new perspective is not speculative. It will be demonstrated to be a synergism of widely accepted concepts of human biology and psychology. We will not take credit for the founding principles. We merely offer an assembly of previously accepted principles which suggest an important perspective on the construct of human personality and the driving force in human behavior.

Freud

Popular perceptions of Freudian psychology seem to focus on his obsession with sexuality. We might observe that Freud's obsession with sexuality was his own neurosis. One might find it academically amusing to observe that Freud's obsession with sexuality is a clinical illustration of his assertion that our present perceptions are strongly influenced by our formative history. He was his own best example of his theories of behavior. But we must not "Throw the baby out with the bathwater". We would argue that his contribution to the study of human behavior was the observation that behavior which is "hysterical" or inappropriate to present circumstance is rooted in the history of the individual. We now know that some hysteria or incongruent behavior is also rooted in biological abnormalities in brain chemistry. However, the essential idea which survives is that childhood experiences have a profound effect on adult behavior. Freud's observation that experiences of the past have a strong influence on attitudes and behaviors in the present survives today and is a founding principle in the studies of human behavior. (Freud, 1893)

Piaget

Later, Piaget described the manner in which personality is constructed by the experiences of the child. Piaget and Inhelder (1969) is a brief essay on these ideas. Specifically, there are three aspects of Piaget's ideas which are essential here. First is the idea that personality is put down in "layers". That it, the development of personality is a linear sequence, to some extent. That is, facial recognition is a skill which is acquired early. If there is little stimulation by exposure to faces at this specific point in development, the subsequent adult individual might have a durable aspect of personality in which there is difficulty in recognizing faces or understanding facial expressions. Second is the idea that the earliest learned concepts and behaviors are basic building blocks of personality. That is, like the foundation of a building, defects in the foundation foster defects in the overall structure. Third is the idea that early learning experiences and attitudes are more durable than later ones.

> ... mental development during the first eighteen months of life is particularly important, for it is during this time that the child constructs all the cognitive substructures that will serve as a point of departure for his later perceptive and intellectual development... (Piaget & Inhelder, 1969, p.3)

Harlow

We mentioned it earlier, but it is important to recall how Harlow, Dodsworth, & Harlow (1965) conducted what might be seen today as a cruel experiment with young Rhesus monkeys. Their expressed intent was to discover how important parental attention and affection was to young monkeys. Young monkeys who were separated from their parents often suffered a permanent social handicap. They were unable to associate with others of their kind, and suffered debilitating anxiety. If we were to pause here, our perspective might stall at: "Of course, parental abandonment is correlated with addiction where the substance is used to kill the anxiety." But if we stopped here, we would not come to the core reason for the anxiety and, therefore, the solution.

Darwin

We mentioned Darwin before. However, just as we amended and clarified Maslow (1943), we must call attention to and amend some of the assertions made by Darwin. Darwin (1893) is recalled in popular circles as describing the idea "Survival of the Fittest". This is a partial truth. What Darwin suggested is the survival of the fittest GENES. It is not the individual which survives; it is the genes, or the best gene pool. This idea is important to our understanding of human behavior. The behavior of the individual will serve to support the survival of the best genes, even if that means sacrifice of the individual. Darwin's basics were expanded upon by others.

Robert Wright

Notably, I must use the first and last name for Mr. Wright (no pun intended) It is interesting observe that wide acceptance and notoriety is evidenced by referring to one by just the surname. We can refer to Freud, Darwin, and Maslow by their surname. Mr. Wright has not yet achieved such notoriety as to be recognized by his surname. Wright's (1994) Work *The Moral Animal* expounded upon the psychology and behavior which is based in genetics. His work brought to light the idea that much more of our behavior is based in genetics than previously thought. The primary purpose of the human individual is not "survival of the individual". The concept of the individual as primary is largely a Eurocentric, agrarian/manufacturing social perception. Wright (1994) examines genetically induced psychology, supporting the idea that behaviors which are harmful to the self might be based in low self-concept. We will discuss contrasting cultural perceptions later, to illustrate this idea.

Sagan

Carl Sagan, who is best known for his "Cosmos" writings and television program, offers his book: *Dragons of Eden* and *Shadows of Forgotten Ancestors* (Sagan & Druyan, 1992). Both of these works offer colorful anecdotes and descriptions of human behavior. His works are more popular and colorful than Wright (1994) but the conclusions are the same: The primary motivator of human beings is NOT the survival of the individual, but the survival of the family (gene pool).

Yates

All of this dialogue comes together in the profound and seminal studies and writings of dedicated academics such as Tuppet Yates (2009) where child neglect or reduced care for the infant has the propensity for long term negative behavioral consequences, to wit:

> "Maltreatment negatively influences developmental processes across multiple levels, including the self-system (e. g, self-other distinctions, body image, self-representation), affect regulation and impulse control (e. g, behavior toward self and others)" (p. 118).

Tuppet M. Yates (2009) refers to this propensity for self-destruction as "Non-Suicidal Self Injury" (NSSI). I offer a small sample of her scholarly work on the topic:

> "A representational pathway toward NSSI holds that maltreatment causes or exacerbates negative representations of the self, of others, and of the self in relation to others that, in turn, contribute to self-injurious outcomes. As described previously, exchanges in the early caregiving relationship lay the foundation for children's core beliefs about self-worth and self-efficacy, expectations of others' responsiveness and care, and general schemas of relationships as safe and nurturing or dangerous and hurtful. "(p. 123)

A summarization of our discussion on self-esteem brings us to the assertion that addiction for some people is self-destructive behavior which is fostered by the developmental environment. The developmental environment has the ability to send a message of low personal self-worth. The result of this perception of low value to the family, the individual might embark upon a pathway of self-injury or destruction.

If the profound value of this idea is not evident to the reader, we suggest that:

I. It clearly explains behavior which otherwise defies logic,
   a. Cutting.
   b. Returning to addiction with full knowledge of the adverse results.

c. Returning to abusive marital circumstances.
   d. Engaging in dangerous behavior, such as risky sports.
   e. Self-humiliation through prostitution or promiscuity.
   f. Outrageous personal attire or hair styles
   g. Highly suggestive or inappropriate dress.
   h. Re-victimization.
II. The concept suggests addiction interventions.
   a. Discourages fear based therapy i. e. "…if you drink, you will die…" (thought: isn't that the point?)
   b. Shifts the focus from the substance or behavior to the underlying pathology.
   c. Suggests nurturing and caring interventions as alternative to controlling and punishing.
   d. Discourages detachment (abandonment) in search of a "bottom".

Conclusion

As promised at the outset, this discussion of self-esteem and addiction has provided an "aha" moment. The apparently "insane" acts of anorexia and cutting can now be better understood. How can one express the intense feeling of grief when observing an adolescent or young adult woman who cannot feed herself, or stop cutting unless she can find some drugs to stop the emotional pain? Somehow it seems more tragic when our loved one is so innocent. It is hoped that this academic presentation which borders on the dry and clinical will, nevertheless, serve to improve our ability to serve these innocents. A summary of this perspective on self-esteem:

Self-Esteem

I. Self Esteem is the individual's measure and perception of his or her value to their perceived family.
   a. This self-perception is a result of a complex process of interpreting a variety of stimuli which contribute to this cumulative measure of personal value.
      i. Parental Care

ii. Praise or criticism by authority
  iii. Personal actions and perceptions of personal value to the family
  b. The individual will manifest rewards, or self-care as a result of a positive perception of personal value to the family.
  c. The individual will manifest or impose punishment, self-deprivation, self-effacement, self-injury, or self-destruction in the event of perceived low self-worth to the family.

II. The perception of the family is rooted in the genetic propensity to support the gene pool even to the detriment of the individual.

III. The perceived family is a flexible social concept in which a person's perception of gene pool or family can be altered by induction into a new family.
  a. Induction into armed forces (Unit, Corps, God, Country)
  b. Recovery fellowship (AA, NA, CA, AL-ANON, CODA)

IV. The construct of self-worth or self-esteem is only partly a cognitive operation or concept.
  a. Cognitive Therapy, while it is helpful, is more effective if it is used with behavior modification which has more power to foster a substantial shift in self-concept.
  b. Self-concept is constructed from the assimilation of human experiences. Therefore, substantial alteration of the self-concept requires human experiences which serve to argue for higher personal value to the perceived social unit (gene pool). i. e.: service to others, personal achievement, social bonding with other members, conformity of dress, language, and behavior. (Feeling connected).

Intervention

Therefore, the religious, or spiritual experience is one in which a shift in self-esteem is created. But this self-concept must be accurate. That is, saying "I'm a good person" has a temporary effect. Affirmations and cognitive therapy are of benefit. However, if the individual does not achieve a profound shift in personal behavior, he or she will preserve a self-concept of low social value and preserve the propensity for self-harm. The value of behavior modification and service to others helps to explain the function and value of grass roots recovery.

Feelings

A clinical understanding of the central nervous system and the limbic system in the human brain is important to the understanding of addiction for professionals. For our purposes, an observation of the sensations and behaviors which are influenced by feelings need not be so clinical. Therefore, the following observations on feelings are designed to create a link between addiction and what is suggested as the driving force in all human behavior and, therefore, in addiction: feelings.

The pure clinician might observe that the discussion here contains some clinical understatements or inaccuracies. However, the following model of human feelings is offered solely for the purpose of wrapping our minds around the complex role of feelings in addiction. We will divide feelings into two categories; emotions and sensations. The two are interrelated and have some influence on each other. In addiction studies, however, the separation of the two enables us to describe two distinct pathways to addiction.

Sensations

It is not difficult to observe that physical sensations influence behavior. When one touches something hot, there is an automatic response to pain where the extremity is withdrawn rapidly in response to the pain. This is offered to illustrate that sensations influence behavior. The human mind, on both a conscious and an intuitive level, associates the sensation of pain or ecstasy with the circumstance which created them. This memory of sensation, associated with the accompanying circumstance influences future behavior based upon experiences of the past. The greater the sensation, (good or bad) the more powerful is the influence.

Emotions

Emotions are sensations, either pleasant or unpleasant which influence behavior in human beings and other animals. Euphoria or Dysphoria is felt as a result of experience. The individual, after an experience, associates the emotions, both on a conscious and on an intuitive level, with the circumstance which surrounded that emotion.

The relationship between emotions and sensations does not have a clear dividing line. The recollection of physical pain, either conscious or unconscious, has the ability to generate the emotions of fear. An example might be a woman who fears a particular man without clearly understanding why when it is a combination of his cologne and his voice which is similar to an early childhood abuser. Her conscious self might not recall the incident, but her intuition associates the sensations of smell and sound with a painful incident of the past.

At this juncture, it is important to observe that feelings serve a valid and essential purpose in life. It is easy to see how important physical pain is to minimize injury. Physical ecstasy is an essential element in insuring that we reproduce, and care for those who are close to us. But it is more difficult and complex to understand the role of emotions.

Briefly, it is important to feel emotions because they are an essential aspect of learning and adapting to life circumstance. In the case of the death of a loved one, the pain of grieving appears to be an essential aspect of adapting to profound change in life circumstance. While grieving can be incredibly uncomfortable, it is widely accepted that the grieving process is an essential element of the ability for the individual to adapt and go forward in life after the loss.

Emotions and Behavior

This discussion will attempt to describe the relationship between the two kinds of choices in behavior. The first is free will. The alternative to free will is that which is instinctive, intuitive, and subconscious or any other choice which is not the result of conscious, logical thought. The human idea that their behavior is, somehow, very different from that of animals seems to exaggerate the belief that we do things out of choice and are not slaves to our feelings, unconscious, or instinctive motivations in our lives. Therefore, the reader is cautioned to be open to the idea that our feelings drive our behavior to a greater extent that we would want to believe.

Emotions as Motivators

Cats are a great example of behavioral pathways (motivations) which are directed by feelings. Somewhere in the makeup of the feline brain is a mechanism which creates euphoria when they chase anything that moves. From the very beginning, we see that feline species enjoy pouncing upon things that move. Clearly, this is an essential aspect of their ability to survive and might be described as a durable characteristic of cats.

Emotions and Association

The human infant is one of the most helpless of all newborn creatures. They do, however, have the tendency to turn the head and suckle when touched on the cheek. Having found sustenance, the little groans of pleasure when suckling are clear indications of the pleasurable sensation thus derived. It is relevant to note that the infant, very early on, opens his or her eyes and gazes upon the face of the mother while experiencing the euphoria of feeding and feeling nourished. Very early, we "associate" the face of the mother with the pleasant sensation of feeding and a full tummy.

This phenomenon of associating feelings with particular stimuli is employed in advertising where a visual image and music which evokes pleasure becomes associated with a product. People then purchase merchandise partially as a result of the pleasant feelings which are associated with the presentation of a logo, a package, or a smell. This suggests that feelings are not merely important to behavior, but that they are an essential element to behavior.

Behavioral Pathways

Imagine yourself attempting to return to a location which you have only visited once before. Recalling the general direction, you arrive at a crossroads or intersection. Gazing at your alternatives, you get a "feeling" that the correct path is to the right. Upon turning, you recognize a landmark and experience a good feeling that you made the right choice. This is an illustration of a behavioral pathway. Our behavior is directed or influenced by these emotions. It is interesting to note that the concept of "women's intuition" has been a part of the mythology of American culture. While this myth is viewed with skepticism by some, many people cultivate an awareness of this intuitive process and employ it as a valid tool in their daily lives.

The Intuitive Self

The human conscious self has limitations upon its capacity to process information. Just the act of reading the printed word is limited by the capacity to recognize symbols, convert them to ideas, and enter them into the logical processes. In the alternative, the intuitive self can engage in an activity and process the sights, smells, sounds and sensations at a rate which is impossible for the conscious self. The conscious self can add a column of figures. The intuitive self can gaze upon a work of art and experience a phenomenological emotional experience which would confound the intellect.

Therefore, when the traveler arrives at an intersection, the intuitive self has the ability to process the infinite stimuli of sights, sounds, smells, colors and relationships. It then influences the cognitive self with subtle "feelings" in a manner to increase the likelihood of making the appropriate choice.

Even the process of adding a column of figures is influenced by the intuitive self where, once a person has identified a goal of any kind, the intuitive self produces a desire to achieve the goal, and induces euphoria upon its completion. This is never more evident than in the case of video games. We, clearly, see that it is just a game, but the process of identifying a goal and struggling to achieve it can be irresistible. Few would deny that the propensity for entering into and completing any game is directed by emotion.

If we return to the illustration of the propensity for cats to chase anything that moves, we note that the act of play in kittens and other young animals mocks the adult survival behavior. The mother Cheetah, at some stage in the development of her young brings home a live animal. This act enables the young to create the association between moving things and food. Thus the behavioral pathway is learned where the adult cheetah, feeling hunger, begins its obsession with moving things and commences the hunt.

Behavioral Pathways and Addiction

Clearly, the description of behavioral pathways explains some aspects of habitual behavior, but it seems inadequate to explain the profound ability of addiction to persuade behavior which causes misery, insanity and death. That is because addictive pathways have additional elements which transform them from the ability to influence behavior to the ability to commandeer absolute control over the addict. There is no one influence over behavior which has the power to remove the capacity for self-determination. It is a combination of factors which increase the propensity for addiction.

Positive and Negative Reinforcement

Consider for a moment the penguin hatchling. The mother and chick bond quickly where the mother offers food and comfort while they memorize the smell and sound of each other. This is positive reinforcement where the euphoria of feeding is associated with the mother. If mother and chick are separated, the chick, when hungry will seek out its mother within the breeding colony. If the chick approaches the wrong adult, he or she will be punished and rejected. This is negative reinforcement which might persuade the chick to stop searching. The question is: How much stronger must positive reinforcement be to persuade the chick to keep searching? The answer is that the positive reinforcement must be infinitely stronger. The chick must keep searching or die.

Such is the power of addiction. The positive reinforcement causes the addict to ignore increasing negative consequences in search of the euphoria or medicinal effect of their substance or their behavior.

For the addict, however, there is an additional component of compulsion. It is withdrawal. In addition to the seeking euphoria, there is the avoidance of withdrawal. These two factors combine to construct obsession and compulsion which is profoundly different and more powerful than mere hunger or desire.

The Stroop Effect

In 1935, J. R. Stroop (1935) conducted a simple experiment. In his experiment, he had subjects read a list of words which were the names of colors: Red, yellow, green, etc. Each subject was timed and the time it took to read the list was recorded. Then the subject was handed an identical list, but this time the words were written in colors. But the color of the word "RED" was written in blue. The color "BLUE" was written in yellow. The result was that reading the second list was visibly more difficult and took a longer time to read. The conclusion was that one part of the brain can interfere with the function of another part of the brain.

The relevance to addiction is that behavioral addictions such as gambling, anorexia, or obsessive disorders can have the capacity to block painful memories. Focusing on some activity can block the processing of painful thoughts or emotions.

We will note later how addiction can be a method of blocking pain, emotional or physical. That is why we often describe behaviors as addictions, similar to substance abuse.

Notably in recovery, the argument over using and attempts to control the addict can successfully block the observation of the real problem. That is, addiction can be used to block painful memories, past or present. In recovery, the addicted person can engage in arguments with family, friends, or clinicians about their substance abuse in an attempt to avoid getting at the core emotional issues which influence the onset of addiction in the first place.

Propensity for Addiction

In an attempt to wrap our mind around the complexities of addiction, we will divide it into stages: Propensity, Progression, Crisis, and Recovery. As we have noted, there is an apparent consensus that addiction is multi-faceted. The use of the "bio psychosocial" intake evaluation for addiction alludes to this idea. We might observe that the term itself, bio psychosocial, suggests a complexity which defies description. We, on the other hand, see it as a suggestion that we examine the whole person, and that the structure of addiction is infinitely complex. This does not suggest that it cannot be understood, but that addiction is as unique as the individual personality. Therefore, we will examine the entire life cycle and the entire person in our attempt to describe addiction.

It is also important to note that the term "propensity" has been carefully chosen. It bears repeating here that addiction is not the result of any singular factor or event. Addiction is the result of a combination of factors which, in their entirety, unite to so influence the individual that they lose the capacity for self-determination. Therefore, we will examine many of the factors which make up human personality and divide them into a time line which alludes to the progression toward the "tipping point" where stresses overcome the person and they become addicted. Thereafter, we will look at the crisis and/or intervention as the reverse tipping point and the beginning of the recovery process. We will begin by examining the genetic influences on the personality which might increase the propensity for addiction.

In addition, we reject the clinical term "risk". This is to reflect the concept that addiction might be the only available means of coping with particularly difficult circumstances. It might be observed that both clinical prescriptions and overt pursuit of psychotropic substances might serve a valid purpose. The presence of a prescription can be just as harmful as illicit purchase of drugs. Likewise, there are circumstances where there is no prescription, but the therapeutic value might, nevertheless be present. An example of substance abuse which serves a valid purpose might be the 8 year old girl who steals alcohol from her grandmother as a means of coping with her chronic sexual abuse by her uncle. Our perspective will continue to avoid passing judgment on the presence of addiction.

Addiction Propensity—Biological

Genetics

We will examine two genetic factors which exercise some influence over the propensity for addiction. One is the genetic propensity which limits the processing of addictive substances. The other is genetic factors which increase the stresses of life and, therefore, increase the probability that the person will look to chemicals for relief from these stresses.

Asbury, Ketcham, Schulstad, & Ciaramicoli (2000) focus on alcoholism. They point, however to both of these genetic factors. First, they describe how some people process alcohol differently than others. Alcohol, for such people, is processed so differently, that the euphoria thus produced is similar to the effect of heroin on other people. The argument is that, for some people, the ability to drink alcohol socially is highly improbable.

Next, they describe how some people are born with a brain chemistry which limits their ability to just feel "OK" under normal circumstances. Such people will have a higher likelihood of using a mood or mind altering substance to manage their emotions.

This brain chemistry might be so unique as to create a mental disorder such as bipolar disorder. Such mental disorders increase the likelihood of using psychotropic substances. This correlation between mental disorders and abuse of addictive substances was described earlier. However, it is important to note that the same medications which might become an aspect of addiction are largely responsible for people with mental illness gaining the ability to be productive members of society. Some of these people, before the advent of modern medicine, might have been institutionalized, or victims of their own destructive behaviors, including suicide.

It is important to note here, also, that Inaba & Cohen (2004) emphasize that mood and mind altering substances serve a legitimate purpose in human society throughout history. Therefore, we must be clear that those who might have a genetic propensity to use alcohol to relax, or caffeine to get them going are not, in themselves addicts, or defective in any manner. The variety of personalities in the human species is an essential element of humanity. Therefore, we repeat that there is nothing inherently wrong with the genetic propensities described. Nor do they condemn these people to addiction. These genetic propensities do not cause addiction, but coupled with other factors, they might contribute.

Prenatal & Perinatal

"Children exposed to maternal drug and alcohol abuse, whether gestationally or after birth are considered at higher risk for cognitive, psychomotor and emotional development disorders" (Nardi, & Delunas, 2000, p. 411). While this clinical observation is relevant, the following extended excerpt from a clinical study is likely to evoke a more emotional response in the reader. This is from a clinical study on the development of the newborn children whose mothers used cocaine during pregnancy.

> "The presence of a newborn infant who seems content when held, feeds well and sleeps well, and has awake periods for getting acquainted with loved ones brings joy to nurses in the newborn nursery as well as to his or her new family. But the presence of a child who is frequently irritable and crying, who is relatively inconsolable and stiff when being held, who has irregular sleeping patterns and wakes up hungry after sleeping only for short periods, and who avoids eye contact and responds poorly to environmental stimuli is quite likely

> to affect his or her caregivers, both nurses an parents, in a negative way. If it is difficult for the nurse to care for this infant in a loving way, how much more difficult it must be for the mother who is already stressed by her craving for cocaine." (Thurman & Berry, 1992, p. 35)

From personal experience, this description of the infant who is discontent as a result of prenatal cocaine use by his or her mother is an essentially accurate description of an infant whose mother abused alcohol. As distressing as the reader might find this description, the actual experience of attempting to console an inconsolable suffering infant is profoundly distressing. Even the memory of the infant's suffering evokes profound sadness. In one such longitudinal study, the infant who suffered withdrawal from alcohol as a newborn blacked out for three days the first time she drank wine, suffered an extended cocaine addiction, conceived an unwanted child while high on marijuana, and eventually lost her license after her third DUI.

At a minimum, our understanding of tolerance, where the chemistry of the body and brain are altered as a result of the use of drugs and alcohol argues that the physiology of the infant whose mother used drugs or alcohol while pregnant has been altered. The further knowledge that recovering persons need a continuing program of recovery suggests that these alterations in brain chemistry and physiology are either permanent or durable. We might conclude that an infant whose mother used drugs during pregnancy is at a higher probability for addictive reactions to mood and mind altering substances later in life.

The use of drugs and/or alcohol during pregnancy increases the propensity for addiction in later life for the unborn child.

Propensity for Addiction—Psychological

Infancy

It is interesting to note that our discussion of the effect of prenatal substance abuse by a pregnant mother brought us to the description of cocaine withdrawal in newborns and how their behavior might reduce the amount of affection and care they receive. This observation suggests that the progress toward addiction has few clear dividing lines.

As noted, the behavior of an infant, if affected by prenatal substance abuse by a parent, can affect how caregivers react to the child. Because this interaction with the parents or other caregivers is essential to the construct of the human personality, the effect of prenatal substance abuse will carry over into infancy. This and other factors serve to foster a limited ability to cope with the challenges of life and, consequently, a higher propensity for substance abuse as a means of coping.

Infants Born Addicted

We have already discussed and described the tension created in the caregiving to an infant who is born to a mother who is abusing addictive substances. Long term effects upon the ability of the child and adult to cope with life are supported by the Harlow, Dodsworth, & Harlow (1965) experiments where young monkeys who were separated from parents had long term social problems. Further, Yates (2009) describes how a lack of care in infants imposes upon the personality a perception that they do not deserve to be nurtured both in infancy and in later life.

Physically, the infant who is born addicted and in withdrawal is argued to be already altered in the physical structure of the brain. They become susceptible to addiction in later life by virtue of the brain's adaptation to the addictive substance as described in the concept of tolerance and progression of addiction.

Mood Altered Caregivers

The action of mood and mind altering substances upon human behavior argues that a parent who is drinking alcohol or using other mood and mind altering substances will be behaviorally altered in a manner which we might call "emotionally unavailable". In the development of human personality, the intense social interaction between the infant and the caregivers is seen as an essential element to the construct of human personality. Attachment theory is widely accepted and:

> "It has an exceptionally strong empirical base and provides a life span developmental framework often absent in current treatment models. Attachment theory focuses on the need for proximity to a sensitive caregiver

in childhood who provides a sense of security and a safe base from which to explore. (Connors, 2011, abstract)."

Parents who are using substances, or in early recovery will be hindered in their ability to provide nurturing care for the infant. This hinders the development of the infant's personality, and affects the ability to cope, in later life. It is argued that this will increase the propensity for addiction as a means to cope, in light of the hindered ability to function effectively.

Birth Defects

A child who displays congenital behavioral abnormalities might be provided inadequate nurturing, and, as a result, feel isolated or disconnected. Notably, it is also possible that a child with physical or mental challenges might receive a positive social reaction to their difficulties and receive more nurturing or focus from caregivers. The result might be a confident, well-adjusted child as a result of the increased focus on care.

Early Childhood Trauma

Profound illness or physical trauma in infancy might have an effect on the construct of personality and, subsequently, the ability of the individual to cope with everyday life. While Yates (2009) describes the relationship between childhood trauma and self-destructive behaviors, it is relevant to describe some of the specific results of different types of trauma.

Child Abuse

Child abuse of all kinds increases the propensity for addiction in adolescence and adulthood. While onset of addiction might appear to be in adolescence, we might note that more than one child reports the onset of substance abuse as a method of coping with abuse. One male reports that claiming illness was a means of coping with early sexual abuse by obtaining medications such as strong antihistamines which induced drowsiness and sleep as a means of escape. Another woman was abandoned by her caregiver at the age of four, left to a profoundly physically abusive parent, and subject to sexual abuse by a male neighbor. She reports stealing wine from her grandmother continuously from the age of 6 as a means to cope with her circumstance.

This tendency to cope with the painful emotions by the use of mood and mind altering substances is observed by Lee, Lyvers, & Edwards (2008). They also suggest that childhood sexual abuse appears to have a greater adverse effect upon female survivors, with the noted observation that there is no apparent correlation between childhood sexual abuse and adult substance abuse in men.

Fitzpatrick, et al. (2010) offer a comprehensive study of the effects of child maltreatment, including sexual abuse. The relative severity of different types of abuse is examined, noting that sexual abuse by a parent produces the most serious adverse effects. Sexual abuse produces the most serious ill effects, (including addiction) followed by physical abuse, and then emotional abuse.

Sexual abuse is correlated with a propensity for substance abuse (Roberts, Nishimoto, & Kirk, 2003). This writer has clinical experience in which sexual abuse on a child can result in anger toward the parent, especially the mother for failing to protect the child. Sexual abuse by a parent has a compound effect upon the child. The abuse imposes the perception that they are of low personal worth by virtue of the deliberate imposition of harm by one who should be a caregiver. Yates (2009) asserts that this self-concept can result in compulsive self-injurious behavior, including substance abuse. Parental sexual abuse also imposes upon the child a perception that those in authority are dangerous and not to be trusted.

Early Parental Loss or Abandonment

There is a correlation between early parental loss and addiction. (Tennant, & Bernardi, 1988). Mishne, (1984) corroborates the idea and suggests that parental loss from death, divorce, or illness have similar effects. It might be observed that, for a child, any absence of a parent or caregiver is perceived as abandonment. The experience of this writer includes a number of self-disclosed onset of habitual alcohol consumption at the loss of a parent. It was observed that the narrative of parental loss emphasized the intense sorrow and the relief provided by alcohol. Notably, the early parental loss and the onset of habitual alcohol use served to dull the personality and interfere with the process of maturity in adolescence. This stunting of emotional growth is seen as an aspect of the progression of addiction.

Physical Trauma

It is not difficult to observe that the trauma which we have described here creates a sense of low self-worth in the child. We might label this as "shame". More difficult to observe is the sense of low self-worth as manifested by physical trauma to the child. It is with great caution that we observe the idea that some religions suggest an intervening deity who rewards good deeds and punishes the wicked. For a child who is the victim of a profound personal injury, there might be created a self-perception that "God doesn't love me." Without threatening the belief system of any reader, it is observed that the shame produced by profound childhood illness or injury can manifest itself in self-destructive behaviors. To recognize this possibility is important in the understanding of addiction. Therefore, the nurturing of a child who suffers from profound injury or illness might include an assertion that interferes with the idea that God is punishing the child. Likewise, recovery from addiction for the survivor must include a process which clearly interferes with the idea that bad things happen to bad people.

Loss of a Sibling

A man who has been struggling to recover from alcoholism for many years displays shame and guilt. Almost incidentally, he relates how, at the age of 9, he was holding his 6 year old brother's hand while waiting to cross a busy street. Suddenly, his brother broke loose, ran in front of a car and was killed in front of his eyes. The children's mother, in horror, screamed that he should have held on tighter.

In the same room sits another man attempting to recover from alcoholism. When queried about his past, relates how he, his younger brother, and his mother were on a bus when the two boys got into an argument. His younger brother was relocated to another seat. An accident ensued in which the younger brother was the only fatality. The idea is that, if he had not argued with his brother, the tragedy would not have occurred. This is exacerbated by the idea that the mother would tend to mitigate her own guilt by shifting blame to the son.

In both of these cases, there appears a profound sense of responsibility for the death of a sibling. This shame and low self-worth operate to create the perception that one does not deserve to get sober, or be happy. It might be argued that this is more than a cognitive idea. It is a durable internal aspect of the concept of self. It is notable, also, that this sense of guilt and propensity for self-injury is stronger where the individual has a propensity for kindness. In famine, the most loving die first, giving their food to those that they love. Likewise, in observing self-destruction through addiction, it is often those of kindest nature who suffer the most.

This description of the guilt as a factor which influences self-destructive behavior is important. Later we will discuss recovery in terms of the "spiritual experience". We might describe this alteration in personality as a "paradigm shift" to be more logical. But the occurrence of guilt and shame as two separate ideas will suggest two separate interventions.

Summary

There are two important reminders here. First, this is not a complete list of the factors which might increase the propensity for addiction. The overall premise is that addiction pathology is as unique to the individual as is individual personality.

Second is the idea that none of these factors CAUSE addiction. Our position is that there is no single cause. No one is to blame. Addiction is the result of an accumulation of factors which influence the propensity for the loss of "The individual capacity for self-determination".

Propensity for Addiction—Sociocultural

Poverty and Racism

The relationship between environment and the development of the human personality has been examined by Urie Bronfenbrenner. A casual look at Bronfenbrenner & Evans (2000) or Bronfenbrenner (1986) offers a discussion of the "Ecology of Human Development".

For our purposes, this offers a widely accepted perspective on how the environment influences the development of the individual. Several observations are of greatest importance to our discussion of the propensity for addiction.

1) Bronfenbrenner (1986) examines and supports the idea that the environment on many levels (family, school, economic environment, religious affiliation, social status) has a marked

effect upon the personality of the individual. This is intended to support our assertions that environment has a profound effect upon the propensity for addiction.

2) Bronfenbrenner (1986) also is clear in asserting that the influences of all the environments are not absolute. That is, the relationship with the environment is a system, where the individual response to the environment is an essential part of the developmental system. In the discussion of addiction, it reiterates that influences are not absolute. No one factor "causes" addiction. The individual has some level of ability to adapt to any environment. Outcomes are not dictated by the environment, but they are influenced by it.

3) An examination of Bronfenbrenner's ideas will reinforce the idea that those influences which carry the most weight are those which are closest and earliest. An example is the idea that the infant relationship with the mother is substantially more influential than the relationship with the 6th grade "shop" teacher.

4) "... intrafamilial processes are affected by extrafamilial concerns..." The social or economic status of the family will have an effect upon the family, and, therefore, the individual. This argues that poverty or social status will have an effect upon the propensity for addiction.

This is offered as evidence and support for the observation that the environment of the child influences the propensity for addiction. Earlier, we spoke of Inaba & Cohen's (2004) observation that mood and mind altering substances have served a historical purpose in survival by enabling human beings to cope with stress. Wadsworth, et al. (2008) link this management of stress with the propensity for substance abuse in the case of poverty and dangerous social atmospheres. The same study (Wadsworth, et al., 2008) asserts the correlation between poverty and cultural drug use.

The preceding offers clear evidence that a culture of poverty and social oppression will increase the propensity for substance abuse and addiction. As we observe the cultural attitudes toward addiction and our social tendency to stigmatize the addict or alcoholic, this evidence of the cause and effect relationship between poverty and addiction suggests that stigmatizing the addict or alcoholic is social oppression, akin to and related to racism.

We might now observe that poverty is a legacy of slavery and racism and that the social isolation of immigrants to the U. S. is similar social oppression. Therefore, we might argue that the propensity for addiction in minority children and adults is partly a result of social oppression and, therefore, more clearly a social issue than an issue of the individual. That is, some addiction could be argued to be a relatively direct result of racism and social oppression in our country. This would call for more direct involvement and responsibility of our social order to assist in the recovery of alcoholics and addicts.

For our purposes here, however, suffice it to say that the propensity for addiction in the individual can be exacerbated by poverty, racism, and social oppression. (Bolland, et. al, 2007)

Behavioral Imprinting

One aspect of the early learning experience is to imitate the behavior of the parents. This is true of all higher species. An example of the imprinting which is related to addiction is the phenomenological experience of a child where the use of alcohol is correlated with a phenomenological experience of sights, sounds, smells, and sensations. The cute name of the beverage "cocktail; toddy, G & T" conveys affection for the beverage and gives it a personality. The sound of the bottle opening, the clink of the ice in the glass, the music, low lights are all parts of the memory related to family. The glasses are clinked in a ritual of social bonding. This ritual use of alcohol is imprinted as a relatively durable component of family identity in the child. Therefore, the propensity for a child to drink or smoke is increased dramatically when the parents drink or smoke. When the practice of using alcohol is such a large part of the family life, it is easy to see how the child will accept frequent drinking as being acceptable. Moreover such an environment might result in a child who will vigorously defend his or her right to drink. If we were then to compare the "coming of age" ritual where the adolescent is admitted into adult society with a drink, the behavioral pathway and the propensity to drink or smoke is not remarkable.

One might argue that this imitation is not a powerful motivator. However, this imitation is more than repetition of behavior. It can become a durable aspect of personal identity. Consider for a moment the man whose sense of personal worth as a man includes stereotypical heterosexual norms. For such a man, having a gay son can be devastating. His emotional turmoil is not a moral issue. His emotional trauma is based in a durable perception of his personal self-worth.

This illustrates the power of family tradition and norms on the construction of children's personality, their self-image, and their concept of self-worth. The self-concept is not just a perception which can be changed with logic. The self-concept is a durable aspect of self which is the foundation for all behaviors, morals, attitudes, and perceptions of self-worth. The reader is referred back to the assertions by Piaget & Inhelder (1935) as cited earlier.

Cultural Tradition

Just as a child becomes imprinted with the behavioral ritual and norms of their parents, they can also be imprinted or influenced by the behavioral norms of their culture. Poverty culture, by necessity cultivates a more avid competition for resources and a higher use of mood and mind altering substances. If one is Italian, to drink and appreciate fine Italian food and wine is an important aspect of culture, family unity, and Italian identity. Judaism contains cultural and faith based rituals which contain wine. Irish culture admires the ability and propensity to consume alcohol.

An important aspect of American counter-culture has been the use of cannabis in social settings, partly because of its association with the idea of "dropping out". The cultural acceptance and encouragement of the use of these mood altering substances increases the likelihood of moral acceptance, likelihood of onset, and the construct of denial where it appears acceptable for mainstream society. If "everyone is doing it, there's nothing wrong with it."

This is not to blame a culture for addiction. As stated before: there is no one to blame. This is not a moral issue. Addiction is not caused by one factor. Addiction is a condition of the human experience which is influenced by a variety of separate but related factors.

Progression

When describing addiction clinically, the word "dependent" is used more than addiction. Clinical descriptions for alcohol dependency include the idea that it is a disease which is "… chronic, fatal, and progressive…" A popular description is that it never gets better, only worse. This suggests that the only solution to dependency is complete abstinence. This is consistent with the grass roots idea that sobriety is complete abstinence. This idea is reinforced with the identification of a "sobriety date", or the date of one's last drink. Social power or prestige in grass roots recovery is largely vested in accumulated years from one's last drink. One who has 40 years of sobriety, for example, would be widely revered.

Supported by this widely accepted idea of the progressive nature of addiction, let us examine the nature of progression, divided into its components as suggested by our "Bio-psycho-social-moral" model of addiction.

Progression—Biological

The nature of the biological progression of addiction is rooted in the idea of tolerance. "… if the use continues over a long period of time, the body is forced to change… The net effect is that the user has to take larger and larger amounts to achieve the same effect…" (Inaba & Cohen, 2004, p. 65)

Nerve cells become less sensitive, and the body's ability to metabolize increases in response to the continued and escalating use. This increase in the ability to cope with a substance creates a competition between the user and his body where larger and larger doses of the drug are required in order to achieve the desired effect. Notably, while the effective dose increases dramatically, the fatal dose increases only marginally. For example, an initial dose of 2 milligrams is a far reach from the fatal dose of 10 milligrams in a drug. After some time and tolerance, the preferred dose has now increased to 10 milligrams, while a fatal dose has only increased to 12 milligrams. This margin is clearly dangerous. A small error in dosage can be fatal.

Notably, if the person taking 10 milligrams were to get clean for say, 90 days and relapsed, their tolerance would have decreased. Their desired dose of 10 milligrams might now be a fatal dose. This explains the higher propensity for fatal overdose in relapse.

In addition to tolerance, which is a physiological defense response, there is physical damage to the central nervous system and the internal organs from the continued and escalating use of drugs and/or alcohol. This idea is so evident and widely known that academic support is not needed herein. But we must expand this discussion to note that behavioral addictions have escalating adverse biological effects. Eating disorders have multiple adverse effects on the body. For example 20% of people suffering from anorexia will prematurely die from complications related to their eating disorder, including suicide and heart problems (Sullivan, 1995).

Progression—Psychological

The psychological aspects of progression are a bit more complex. In addition, the understanding of human behavior itself harbors more mystery. Because of this complexity, a complete review of the psychological aspects of the progression is impossible here. We will offer adequate information to illustrate and support the idea that the progression of addiction has profound psychological forces and, therefore, argues for psychological interventions in recovery.

Hindrance of emotional development—In grass roots recovery, one will often hear the somewhat mythological idea that if one began drinking alcohol at the age of 18, their emotional development is stunted at that level. The idea is that the newly recovering alcoholic is, emotionally, 18 when they stop drinking.

While this is an exaggeration with a valid purpose of making recovery dialogue interesting, mental health professionals might agree that there is some truth to this idea. Inaba & Cohen (2004) comment that: "The use of psychoactive drugs can delay users' emotional development and keep them from learning how to deal with life's problems." (p. 494). In seeking support for this idea, however, this author found more evidence that substance abuse was a result of stunted emotional development. Notably Armstrong & Costello (2002) in a review of the literature on the topic concluded that "Child psychopathology… was associated with early onset of substance use and abuse in later adolescence." (Abstract). Therefore, emotional immaturity, or a limited ability to cope is related to substance abuse in adolescents. Which one caused the other is not clear. However, the premise that substance abuse is a coping mechanism argues that the continued substance abuse in adolescence interferes with the educational process and socialization. This interference with social and emotional development, increases stress and, therefore, increases the need for substances to cope.

Suppression of painful memories—We might note that the processing of life experiences into the human personality is a critical process. As previously noted, survivors of childhood trauma have a higher likelihood of substance abuse as a means of coping with the trauma. It has also been noted that the likelihood of re-victimization is higher among substance abusing survivors. This re-victimization during substance abuse heaps more painful memories upon the survivor. These additional painful memories will increase the need for more substances in order to cope. With time, the use of psychotropic substances to block painful emotions also blocks the emotional processes. As a result, when the addict attempts abstinence, this accumulation of unresolved emotional issues seems to explode into the consciousness, causing overwhelming fear and anxiety. It might be observed that the longer one uses, the greater the emotional upheaval when attempting to get clean and sober.

Guilt over Aberrant Behavior—Substance abusers, as the condition progresses, increase their neglect of their responsibilities and can engage in behaviors which are inconsistent with their own moral codes.

Upon awakening, the addict can recall the events of the night before where, hindered in judgment, they behaved in a manner which now brings guilt or shame. With time, such recollections become cumulative. This increase in shame and guilt calls for an increase in the addictive behavior to block the increasingly unpleasant memories. The weight of this guilt and shame can be profound, especially when criminal behavior was involved in the process of obtaining or financing one's habit. If this accumulation of guilt is strong enough, it might cause a profound shift in self-image. The self-concept of being a criminal might propagate behavior patterns of aggression. This pattern of behavior and its effect upon self-concept might be a predictor or creator of habitual criminality.

Blaming Behavior—Blaming behavior or thoughts is one of the apparent characteristics of addiction. It might be argued that the continuing transaction wherein the substance or behavior has profound control over mood suggests that one's feelings come from outside sources. Grass Roots recovery often chants: "It's an inside job." This is an automatic response to the observation that the addict blames things on the outside for how they feel on the inside. These blaming thoughts and behaviors isolate the addict socially. As tolerance for the substance increases, the blaming behavior becomes more overt. With time, the addict/alcoholic actively condemns and criticizes those closest to him. Rejecting others seems rational and logical to the active addict or alcoholic.

Cognitive Impairment—With time, the ability to interact with one's environment deteriorates. The alcoholic who is now drinking throughout the day might appear to be functioning, but is impaired to the extent that others see their behavior as a bit "strange". They can't put their finger on it, but the chronic user seems a bit "off". In addition to this tendency, the continued use of substances can cause subtle physical damage to the cognitive portions of the brain, resulting in subtle limitations in cognitive function. The ability to function continues to deteriorate.

In summary, it is important to note that the progression of the ability to function psychologically does not occur in a linear progression. The progression of this and other aspects of addiction have a cumulative "snowball" effect. It might begin slowly and remain moderate for a long period of time. But it can suddenly gain momentum and collapse like a landslide. A person can appear to hang on for a long period of time when, suddenly, the house of cards collapses. The hope is that the crisis is profound enough to persuade intervention, but not so strong that it causes death, permanent disability, or incarceration.

The person suffering from addiction often speaks of their emotional discomfort to a health care professional. For a variety of reasons, including denial, they will often not be honest about their substance use. With all good intentions, the health care professional strives to reduce the suffering of their patient by prescribing medication. This can accelerate the progression of the disease. Not uncommon is for someone with emotional discomfort related to alcohol consumption to be prescribed a psychotropic substance such as a sleeping aid or anti-anxiety drug. This might create a secondary addiction, accelerate the primary addiction, or the combination of substances might have a synergistic effect and induce a crisis.

Progression—Socio-cultural

It might be seen as redundant to describe the deterioration of addiction socially. We have alluded to it in the psychological portion. However, the descriptions here are intended to offer the opportunity for the addict to see themselves and begin the process of recovery on two fronts. The first is the idea that my family is not the problem. The second is that recovery includes the ability to rebuild my relationship with others where my interpersonal relationships become an asset, rather than a liability.

Deterioration of family—We have already mentioned the tendency of addictive behaviors to interfere with our interpersonal relationships in general. But the relationship with family bears special comment. There is the continuing dilemma of parenting and family support where one level of family support is helpful, but others are harmful.

There is observed the circumstance where a wealthy or financially comfortable family structure sees the reduction of hardship as being one of the benefits of wealth or privilege. However, as we have seen with the untimely death of wealthy celebrities, too much good fortune with little hardship can be harmful or hazardous.

In the case of childhood wealth and privilege, the lack of hardship might undermine the building of character. Without hardship, one might not develop adequate coping skills. The untimely death of the children of wealth might be evidence of this phenomenon. In addition, the family might see the act of posting bond, buying a new car when the last one was wrecked, or fronting the money for defense attorneys to be the responsibility of family and one of the benefits of wealth.

The concept of "detaching" was a relatively early concept in dealing with an addicted family member. The "consequences of our actions" are an important aspect of emotional development. This act of detaching has now evolved into a perspective where the family now sees it as a responsibility to "manifest" crisis in the life of the addict. Intervention is now seen as the responsibility of the family. We will later discuss the profound utility of a crisis as an important moment in the process of recovery.

Therefore, the family becomes a critical component in the progression of addiction. It might be argued that the most loving family is the one who becomes most alienated. The more they attempt to help, the greater is the damage to the family as a result of the addiction. The alcoholic/addict is so obsessed with using that the family becomes emotionally abandoned. The family efforts to help the addict can deplete resources of both money and emotion. The rift between the addict and the family becomes a chasm as the family manifests greater and greater attempts to help and the addict manufactures more reasons to blame the family.

Reduced ability in job production—The employment venue is not substantially different from the family. The addict/alcoholic deteriorates in their ability to produce at work. Like the family, the employer might have a legitimate desire to assist. They might enable the addict, detach, or intervene. The progression of the addictive condition, if not arrested will result in a person who is unemployed and/or unemployable.

Law issues related to driving and incidental crime—From personal experience, it is argued here that, at some point, the alcoholic loses the capacity for self-determination in life. On a micro scale, however, the loss of self-determination when using occurs much earlier. We would define "alcoholic" drinking as a circumstance in which one drink can cause the loss of self-control. We might define one aspect of the alcoholic drinker as the loss of self-control after one or two drinks. For many alcoholic drinkers, if they drink, they WILL drive. When sober, it is easy to see that driving while drinking is hazardous to self and others. After one or two drinks, however, the perception of the alcoholic drinker shifts immediately. They lose the ability to make that determination, and they insist upon driving. The social drinker, when they feel impaired, intuitively knows to ask someone else to drive. The alcoholic drinker, on the other hand, might gain more confidence that they can drive well as they become more impaired.

In grass roots recovery it is often culturally acceptable to describe one's drinking in terms of "number of DUI's" or "number of detox's". This illustrates and affirms the almost unbelievable level of destruction and dysfunction that progression can manifest.

The fortunate person in recovery need only discuss the number of DUI's achieved. Recovery for others is made more difficult when sobriety forces them to recall that their drinking induced behavior caused the death of some innocent child.

This would argue that while one seems to need a "bottom" to get sober, sometimes the "bottom" can be the greatest obstacle to long term recovery.

Criminal behavior related to addiction—The correlation between addiction and the criminal population is easily observed and well documented (DOHHS, 1990).

Our definition of addiction "… loss of the capacity for self-determination…", and the descriptions of progression where relationships, family, and jobs deteriorate offer a clear description of how the increasing desperation of the addict results in criminal behavior. Driving while under the influence, purchasing illegal substances, and stealing to support one's habit, are all aspects of the progression of criminality in addictive progression. Important to this section is the observation that just being arrested once is often not enough to stop the progression. In grass roots recovery, denial that one will become a criminal is often met with the observation that one has not been arrested "… yet…" The clear consensus is that, if one continues to drink and use, none of the most horrible outcomes are impossible. Death, incarceration, or institutionalization as a result of permanent damage to the brain are all seen as the inevitable result of continued use.

Progression—Spiritual/Moral

It is not difficult to observe that the addicted person, if they continue the behavior, will compromise their morality. This deterioration in moral conduct is an element of more than one aspect of progression. The family is shocked at the addictive behavior which is, clearly, not in accordance with how they previously understood the person. Stealing from one's mother, for example might be seen as reprehensible, but is not uncommon for the addicted person.

It might be argued that this decay in moral behavior plays a part in the social stigma which is attached to alcoholism and addiction. The "disease" concept is offered by many in an effort to defuse this social stigma. The idea that one's son has a disease seems to mitigate the emotional distress which is felt by the abused and/or rejected family.

This moral decay is offered here as an essential element in understanding addiction and recovery. We have already observed the guilt felt by the newly clean and sober person when they come to some realization of behavior which is outside of their own conscience or moral code. Therefore, it might be observed that the kindest person might have more difficulty in recovery because of the overwhelming guilt.

It might also be observed that the immoral, criminal, or socially aggressive behavior might have been necessary to survive in the environment of addiction. Therefore, the behavior patterns might be so durable that long term recovery is required in order for the recovering person to learn and adopt behaviors which are more appropriate to mainstream society. To measure and understand the role of morality in recovery, the reader might be referred to the observations of Kohlberg, as describe and summarized in Kohlberg & Hersh (1977).

This observation of the moral deterioration in the progression of addiction has special importance in light of recent observations about the pathology of addiction. Relevant to these new perspectives, two important aspects of morality are offered here:

First is the idea that addiction can be or become an act of self-destruction. Yates (2009) offers a direct correlation between low self-image and the propensity for self-injury. Asbury, Ketcham, Schulstad, & Ciaramicoli, (2000), in their detailed description of alcoholism, pause to observe that the alcoholic often sees the self-destruction of alcoholism as, somehow, deserved.

This idea of the propensity for self-harm related to low self-image, suggests that fear-based interventions can cause harm. That is, to say to the recovering person "... to drink is to die..." will receive the silent internal observation: "... yeah, isn't that the point?..."

Second is the suggestion here that, because the pathology of addiction might contain elements of self-destruction, abstinence as a result of the fear of consequences is tenuous, at best. We suggest that fear, crisis and pain can bring one into recovery. Sustained recovery might require a shift in perspective which contains a moral component. We would offer the apparent requirement of a "spiritual" experience as evidence that there is a moral component to addiction and recovery.

Briefly, we would suggest that each person has a unique conscience, a sense of what is right and wrong. Regardless of the open declarations of one's self-worth, there lies within a conscience which interprets behavior. If the conscience or the self-concept perceives that the person is of low moral standing or low worth as a person, then behavior will be manifest which is appropriate to this self-concept. This includes, in addiction, an increasing tendency toward self-destruction or self-injury (Yates, 2009) as the throes of addiction force behaviors which the self sees as immoral.

Summary

The progression of addiction is manifested in the synergism of factors and a cumulative effect upon the ability to function or cope. It is this "Loss of the power of self-determination" which leaves the addicted person essentially hopeless in the absence of assistance. Further, the denial system of the addicted person marshals all of what little power they have to resist any interference in their behavior.

While the grass roots culture might argue that the person must reach a "bottom", we might temper the idea with the observation that, in the absence of a crisis, there is little hope of recovery. That is, as long as the addict has some level of power, this power will be directed to the preservation of their relationship with their addiction.

Therefore, it is important to observe that crisis is important, while a "bottom" is not necessary. Research has shown that recovery rates for those forced into addiction treatment can be approximately the same as those who go willingly (Kelly, Finney, & Moos, 2004). This relatively new information argues that court mandates to recovery programs can be substantially more productive and less expensive than incarceration.

This brings us to a discussion of crisis and its role in addiction and recovery.

Addiction—Crisis

Crisis—Obstruction

The title of this section is intended to be an apparent paradox in addiction dialogue. But it is necessary to observe that addiction pathology has a social element both in progression and in recovery. This might be most evident where the prevention of crisis for an addict or alcoholic can be fatal.

Parenting

There is a legitimate moral dilemma in parenting. This dilemma is, perhaps most evident in addiction pathology. The moral dilemma is "When am I helping? When am I hurting?"

This dilemma begins very early. The dilemma occurs when a legitimate desire to protect our children becomes excessive, and the child is prevented from learning to deal with adversity. It might be observed that this might be more likely to occur in a family where one or more parents have overcome poverty and become wealthy. The effort to provide a better life results in insulating their children from pain or difficulty. If this does not cause harm in early childhood, such an attitude of over-protecting a child can later cause a parent to remove the consequences of action by: posting bond, hiring attorneys, replacing wrecked cars, and providing unlimited funds.

This is not to condemn the legitimate desire to protect our children. It is to identify one of the legitimate moral social dilemmas of our time and connect it to addiction pathology. Addiction interventions must address this aspect of addiction which we have termed "enabling" behavior. This is where the addict's ability to progress in their disease obtains assistance from well-meaning and loving parents, family members, friends, or business associates.

Wealth and Social Power

At this writing, our country is mourning the loss of Whitney Houston. The trial of a physician to Michael Jackson is recent news. The children of families with great wealth and social power are at increased risk of having such wealth that there is always someone who, for a price, will assist them in their self-destruction. While it is social news, and the public might offer public grief, the sorrow and profound sense of loss which a mother experiences at the loss of her child is no less profound for a woman based upon her social status.

In grass roots venues, the culture observes that "… too much, too good, too soon…" observes that power or success can be a factor in the development of addiction, and a detriment to the ability of the addict or alcoholic to achieve long term recovery. This is done by preventing or postponing an important element in the commencement of recovery.

Therefore, it might be observed that the absence of crisis can be fatal.

Crisis—Importance

In grass roots recovery, the culture creates its own dialogue and terminology. In that venue, there is often dialogue of how recovering people much reach their "bottom". For our discussion, this is one form of crisis, and we will accept that such an occurrence is helpful, but is not always necessary. Grass roots recovery would agree with this observation by their additional cultural observation that "… one can get off the elevator at any floor…"

In clinical venues, we observe that to describe the progression of disease as "inevitable" is only a small exaggeration. In the absence of some event which interferes with the progression, there will be no recovery. The end result of the progression, as suggested in grass roots culture is "… jails, institutions, or death…"

Notably, however, an old sage of reasonable reputation in grass roots recovery once noted that there is another alternative which he terms "… the legion of the lost…". This refers to those for whom addiction takes them to a place of poverty, sadness, and isolation akin to a prison without bars. These are not only the homeless alcoholic in the street, but the person who has successfully created an environment of personal isolation in their apartment or home where they can live out their life in perpetual suffering.

With these observations in mind, we identify the interruption of disease progression with the term "intervention". In the absence of some intervention, the addict/alcoholic who has lost the capacity for self-determination is less like a runaway train which meets with its fate quickly, and more like a huge ship without a rudder. Slowly and miserably with everyone watching in powerless frustration, they defend their right and power of self-destruction.

Therefore, we define addiction in terms of the loss of power of self-determination where the addict/alcoholic expends ever greater amounts of energy in defending their right to self-destruction. As long as the addict possesses enough social power, it can be directed toward the progression of addiction.

Crisis—Biological

Tolerance and Deterioration of Benefit

In a recent intervention, it was necessary to purchase alcohol for a person who needed to drink continuously in order to prevent withdrawal. The tolerance for alcohol had increased until it was necessary to drink constantly in order to prevent withdrawal. The fear of withdrawal was so intense that the person, in between drinks was terrified to be refused admittance to an inpatient hospitalization for detoxification from alcohol. There is a progression of tolerance where increasing amounts of the substance are needed just to stave off withdrawal. The substance begins to lose its ability to provide euphoric or other benefit. This intersection of tolerance and exhaustion of benefit creates a valid crisis.

Deterioration of Reward and Consequences

As noted earlier, the euphoria of using a substance persuades many to use drugs and alcohol. For most people, this reward cascade can be used productively. For the addict, however, tolerance requires more and frequent use. In addition, fear of withdrawal is further motivation to use. With the progression, however, rewards diminish with tolerance. The effort needed to continue use increases, and the symptoms of withdrawal become more intense, and more often. The consequences of use also occur more closely to the use, increasing the perception that the consequences and the use are connected. That is, denial is more difficult when the consequences come more quickly and more often. Therefore, there can be a gradual shift in perception where the ability to maintain a denial system becomes more difficult. This process can result on a "… moment of clarity…" (Another grass roots term). For alcoholics, this process is described as "… alcohol is the final convincer…" (This is the same guy who told me not to quote him.). Just using can, over time, cause a shift in perception on the part of the addict or alcoholic. Another grass roots description is the one where this moment of clarity become a durable perception of addiction: "… once you know you are a fool, you can't be a fool anymore…"

Calamity

A woman speaks at a grass roots meeting and discloses to those present that her last drug use was the night that their home was invaded by drug addicts searching for drugs or money. When they were refused, the invaders shot and killed her 4 year old son.

A man shares the lectern that he got sober in prison. It was his fourth trip to the penitentiary for attempted murder on his wife. He reports that he does not recall the attempt because he was in an alcoholic blackout. In a private conversation, he relates the incident with tears in his eyes. Not because he went to prison, but because he really loved his wife and regrets ever doing anything to harm her.

The preceding stories are relevant on two fronts. They are, first, an illustration of the type of calamity that is profound enough to break the cycle of addiction. Second is the value of grass roots recovery where the story of others hopes to cause the psychic change which breaks the progression of addiction for the recovering persons in attendance.

Whether it is the fourth DUI, serious injury to one's self, or a loved one, or incarceration, calamity can be the crisis which begins the process of recovery.

Physical Illness

Serious physical illness such as liver disease heart disease, alcoholic paralysis, Wernicke-Korsakoff syndrome (Beers, et al., 2006), pancreatitis, gastric ulcers, can all be serious enough to interrupt the progression of addiction.

A newcomer at a grass roots meeting related that his drinking has caused paralysis in his right side. 30 days of abstinence saw some healing of this paralysis and, with the declaration that "it wasn't that bad," he decided that he could drink socially and ceased the recovery process.

Another in recovery spoke at the lectern and related how he was in an alcohol induced coma for two days. Within four hours of discharge from the hospital, he was drunk again.

Broken arms and legs, black eyes, automobile accidents, all are results of the progression of addiction which sometimes bring a person into recovery.

But the capacity for the obsession to induce short memory can be remarkable.

Crisis—Psychological

Deterioration of Function

The progression of addiction or alcoholism erodes the ability of the addict or alcoholic to function in mainstream society. The ability to work productively deteriorates. The ability to deal with mainstream life stresses is part of the progression where more of the substance causes more life problems, requiring more substance to mediate the stress. Sometimes the ability to function causes a crisis. "… lost my job, my wife left me, lost my license…"

Isolation and Depression

With progression, the focus on the addiction increases demands on time and psychic energy. In the absence of productive social interaction, family and friendships deteriorate. Social isolation increases. Those who are addicted to stimulants, or exciting behavioral addictions, such as gambling or sex addiction experience increasing depths of depression between episodes. For those addicted to depressants, such as alcohol, or depressive addictions such as anorexia nervosa, or cutting, the relief between depressive episodes become shorter.

Accumulation of Emotion Process

For some, the function of mood and mind altering substances and behavior were initiated in an effort to cope with profound emotional pain of oppression, abuse, or trauma. As addiction continues, the feelings or circumstances which have not been processed productively will accumulate. For some, the anger accumulates until it can be contained no longer and becomes rage. For others, the sadness accumulates and exacerbates the depression and the accompanying propensity for self-harm, including the propensity for suicide.

This propensity to avoid the processing of feelings causes an increasing, cumulative burden of emotion. This burden of emotion can well up suddenly when the drug or behavior is removed. The psychological progression of addiction is the accumulation of feelings, losses, fears, anger, and anxiety which go unanswered as long as emotional growth is blocked by the substance or behaviors of addiction. Crisis occurs when the accumulation of emotion can no longer be contained by the addictive substance or behavior.

Crisis—Socio/Cultural

Tolerance and Cost; Exhaustion of Resources

As tolerance increases, especially in the case of drugs, the expense involved in maintaining a habit increases the amount of time, energy, and money to support the habit. This economic pressure pushes the addict to a tipping point where they can no longer successfully support their habit. There comes a time when the crisis is that the cost of using outruns the available financial resources.

Criminal Crisis

Those in grass roots recovery are often heard to say: "After my fourth DUI, I knew I needed to change, so I quit driving". This statement is humorous and profound for the person in recovery. It is often seen as insane and illogical to the non-alcoholic. We have already described the relationship between criminality and substance abuse. Therefore, it might be apparent that an addict might be arrested for possession, distribution, paraphernalia, driving while intoxicated, violence under the influence, or violence in search of drugs or money to buy drugs. The statement about quitting driving is intended to illustrate the kind of thinking which is perfectly reasonable to the addict/alcoholic, but makes little logical sense to the rest of us. When we speak of addiction and recovery this apparently irrational thinking makes perfect sense as a symptom of chemical dependency.

The legitimate moral dilemma here is in the definition of a criminal, its relationship to chemical dependency, moral questions, and the propensity for recidivism in both criminal and addictive behavior. At this juncture, where we correlate chemical dependency with our social and criminal system, the social issues come into play when we begin to define interventions. Interventions can merely arrest chemical dependency. However, better interventions can not only arrest suicide by chemical dependency, they can be the start of a recovery process which includes long term remission and an opportunity for re-entry into a productive position in society and a path to self-actualization.

In the case of criminality and chemical dependency, the allocation of resources faces the grim fact that incarceration means greater recidivism, while treatment for chemical dependency can foster recovery.

That being said, it is frequently observed in grass roots venues that: "…prison saved my life…or I got sober in prison…" How about this one: "I was sitting in jail when I thought; maybe if I don't drink…"

For many of the chemically dependent, incarceration is the beginning of recovery. This argues that a law enforcement official faces a dilemma similar to that of other authorities: the parents. The question is: "When am I helping, and when am I causing harm?" When we let a drunk driver off, who are we helping?" The question is not intended to imply an answer. It is a legitimate moral dilemma.

Familial Intervention

If we refer back to the perception by the grass roots culture that one "… must be ready…" or "… must reach a bottom…" we might argue that this was an accurate observation before the advent of legislation. Some state legislation recognizes the idea that one might need an intervention to prevent injury to self or others. In Florida, there is a law which enables law enforcement to forcibly detain an individual who is a threat to themselves or others. There is also a law which enables family members to enforce treatment for a person who is a danger to themselves.

Poverty

In grass roots recovery, it is repeated: "… from Yale to jail… Park Avenue to park bench…" On the other side of the social spectrum are those whose addiction can be exacerbated by the misery of poverty. As the disease progresses, we become unemployable. Physical deterioration makes us socially unattractive. While there are laws against discrimination, there is a stigma attached to the addict or alcoholic in the final throes of poverty. This is true whether the poverty is one of the causes or the result of addiction. The legitimate dilemma here, however, is the idea that, as long as we can function, we continue the addiction. Sometimes the poverty and resulting loss of social power is a tipping point which begins the process of recovery.

Crisis—Spiritual/Moral

If we accept the idea that most persons possess an internal moral code of behavior, it is apparent that the behavioral progression of addiction will create an internal moral conflict. As addiction progresses, the individual first neglects his or her responsibility to one's family, profession and community. In recovery, it is not uncommon for a person to reveal such behavior, first in their personal inventory, and later in open declaration at meeting. It begins with neglect, but progresses to overt larceny to support the addiction. Crisis can come in a moment of clarity where one's actions become so outrageous that denial or suppression of the guilt is no longer effective. If the resulting anguish and guilt do not trigger self-destruction, they might motivate the addict to seek help. This search for assistance might even be subtle, such as allowing one to be caught in the act of stealing. More common might be a confession to a spouse, or a phone call in response to an advertisement on television. For the sake of the addict, it is hoped that overwhelming guilt will result in a cry for help rather than self-destruction.

Summary

In whatever form crisis appears, we suggest that it can be an important aspect in the transition from progression to recovery. An old sage refers to it as "… the moment of truth…" Some suggest that it is "…God is doing for us what we cannot do for ourselves…" (AA, 1976, pp. 83-84). Whatever the case, crisis will be observed to be an essential element in most of the stories told by successfully recovering persons.

Addiction—Recovery

Definition

Our definition of addiction as "… the loss of the capacity for self-determination…" suggests that recovery includes all of the elements which enable a human being to function. That is, in order to regain the ability to function, we must address all of the components and resources which enable one to function. We have identified the "tipping point" where the challenges and stress of functioning have exhausted the resources of the person, and they lose the ability to cope. Therefore, recovery is identified as restoring the ability to function by restoring the personal resources of the person.

Notably, these personal coping mechanisms or resources are the same ones which have been identified as the resources and capabilities of the person who is seeking self-actualization. Therefore, the process of recovery might be seen as a continuum of self-actualization which is a universal aspect of personal growth for all persons.

This process is unique to persons recovering from addiction on at least two fronts. First is the idea that the process begins at a lower level of functioning. Second are the consequences of failure. For the average person, a failure to grow as a person results in mediocrity. For a person in recovery, failure results in death, incarceration, or some similar profoundly tragic result.

Therefore, we suggest that the recovery process is merely the process of personal reflection, self-awareness, self-care and self-actualization with the unique motivation of avoiding the profound consequences of relapse to addiction.

Recovery—Biological

Detoxification or "Detox" is the act of removing the addictive substance from the body. In the case of alcohol, the withdrawal symptoms can be fatal. Therefore, the first step in recovery is removing the substance, or the behavior long enough for the body to begin the physical healing process. This physical recovery, however, does not end here. The physical damage to the human body can be profound. Liver disease is widely recognized as correlated with alcohol abuse. For those who mixed alcohol and cocaine, there was created a third substance "cocaethylene" (Inaba & Cohen, 2004) which causes damage to the heart muscle. Heroin addicts might suffer the loss of teeth. The process of physical recovery can be a long road of healing. Moreover, the self-loathing which often accompanies early recovery is sometimes evidenced by self-neglect. A continuing process of increasing self-care is seen as evidence of the progression in recovery. There are publications which address the peculiar health issues in recovery from addiction. *Eating Right to Live Sober* (Ketcham & Mueller, 1986) addresses the dietary and health issues for those recovering from alcohol abuse, including a notation of the correlation between alcoholism and hypoglycemia.

As we review our definition of addiction where a person has lost the capacity for self-determination, it is important to note that addiction for many is a self-destructive means of coping with stress. Physical health is one of the essential needs of living. Physical health increases the individual's ability to deal with the challenges of life. Therefore, maintaining physical health increases the ability of the recovering person to cope with the normal challenges of life and, therefore, increases the likelihood of maintaining recovery.

Physical health is an essential element of the propensity for addiction. The deterioration of physical health is one of the symptoms of addiction and its progression. Physical health, therefore, is an essential element of recovery.

Recovery—Psychological

When we looked at the propensity for addiction, we identified the idea where lack of care, or profound trauma in childhood manifested itself in a self-concept of low worth, resulting in self-neglect or, in the extreme, self-injury. This self-concept is not created by thoughts alone. The self-concept is a result of what we refer to as a phenomenological experience. It is a life experience which involves all the senses. Being sexually abused, abandoned or neglected as a child is not a thought. It is an experience which impacts the concept of self when the person is most vulnerable and most open to suggestion. As a result, cognitive therapy and affirmations of self-worth, while helpful, do not have the ability to impact the sense of self sufficiently to alter this concept. Moreover, the earlier the experience, the more basic and durable it is to the self-concept. (Bruner & Anglin, 1973, Piaget & Inhelder, 1969, Freud, 1893)

We might refer to this low sense of self as "shame". In the case of survivors of childhood trauma, this sense of self is a lie. That is, the concept of self and one's relationship to the world is inaccurate. As a result, the behavior of that person will be observed as puzzling or incongruent to others.

The capacity to amend the message received in a life experience requires a life experience of equal weight to alter the self-concept. This idea begins to remove some of the mystery surrounding the effectiveness of grass roots recovery. At the core of recovery from alcoholism, drug addiction, and other forms of self-injury is a restoring and restructuring of the self-concept through loving relationships with safe and like-minded persons. These loving relationships and selfless service to others in grass roots recovery is a phenomenological human experience which, when applied over time, serve to amend the self-concept. My dear friend Franklin C., in his unique manner would suggest: "If you want self-esteem, you must perform estimable acts."

There is another aspect of the psychological component of addiction which also manifests itself in emotional discomfort. That one is guilt. As we observe the progression of addiction, we note that the active addict, alcoholic, compulsive gambler, or even the workaholic has behaved in a manner which violates their own internal moral code. When they become aware of their addiction and its effect upon their family, their employers and their friends, there is profound guilt. Notably, this guilt and pain is greater for the person whose internal moral fiber is most pro-social. That is, the person who, in the absence of addiction has the most to contribute to society might be the one who has the greatest pain of guilt and shame upon achieving abstinence.

Notably, upon achieving a short term of abstinence, these people might feel physically better, but their emotions can be profoundly painful. This explains the importance of the 9th step amends (AA, 2001). If the reader now finds this idea of amends to be remarkable, bear in mind that the Catholic Church has cultivated the sacrament of confession for almost two thousand years. As a child, I sat in the church Saturday afternoon and reflected on my wrongs, (step 4); entered the confessional and shared them with God and another human being (Step 5), and practiced the prescribed acts of contrition and penance as prescribed by the priest (Step 9) after praying and meditating in the church (step 11).

It is suggested that this observation of the consistency between the 12 steps and the moral and spiritual principles suggested by others serves to reinforce the value of these practices and their relatively universal acceptance across time and faith.

We might add here that this process is not unique to recovering addicts and alcoholics. This process of self-discovery might be observed to be as basic as the search for self-actualization as described by Maslow (1943) and that striving toward personal self-actualization which is advocated by Rogers (1961). Moreover, this personal inventory as suggested by step 10 was said to be advocated by Pythagoras (yes, the mathematician) where the members of the Pythagorean Society "… At the close of each day they were to ask themselves what wrongs they had committed, what duties they had neglected, what goods they had done…"(Lyra Graeca III, p. 283 as cited by Durant, 1939).

We might further de-mystify and argue the universal application of the 12 steps of recovery by noting the introduction to "12 Steps and 12 Traditions" (AA, 1953) which reads: "A.A.'s Twelve Steps are a group of principles, spiritual in their nature, which, if practiced as a way of life, can expel the obsession to drink and enable the sufferer to become happily and usefully whole." (p.15).

Recovery—Socio-Cultural

"Recovery... involved addressing the sense alcoholics often feel of being unique and isolated." (Miller, 2009, p. 331). Miller suggests that this sense of isolation is partially a result of the declaration by many recovering persons of their "love relationship" with their drug of choice. Grass roots talks from the recovering person often will contain the declaration that abstinence is, in effect, the loss of their best friend. Notably, however, it is often heard: "... I always felt different..." This idea is not argued to be universal, but it is not difficult to observe that a survivor of childhood trauma, the child of alcoholic parents, or a child living in a dangerous, low income neighborhood will feel isolated. Notably, all of the preceding circumstances are correlated with a higher propensity for addiction in adulthood. (Yates, 2009; Lee, Lyvers, & Edwards, 2008).

Now, if we observe the social progression of the addiction, the sufferer becomes increasingly isolated. If they have moved to crime or successive driving offenses related to their addiction, they will come to perceive themselves not only as isolated, but as a pariah to society. They are increasingly wary, and distrustful.

AA (1953) alludes to the progression of social isolation. Whether the addict had no social skills as a result of his or her upbringing, or whether it is a result of long term addiction, the result might be: "We were having trouble with our personal relationships..." (p.52)

The beginning of recovery might be the arrival at a grass roots meeting of AA, NA or other venue. If the new person is fortunate, they will arrive at a meeting which actively recognizes and welcomes newcomers. They will be noticed and gently welcomed. Someone might get them a cup of coffee. They might be introduced and asked to participate. If they are less fortunate, they will be able to quietly enter, sit in the rear, and leave before the meeting ends, thus reinforcing their disdain and fear of recovery.

For others, it is a family, court, or employer intervention which finds them in a facility which treats addiction. The process of socialization begins with the staff at the center. Welcomed, cared for, listened to, and given attention, perhaps for the first time in their life, the paradigm shift begins.

It is at this juncture that it might be interesting to examine the "recovery" concept where it is contrasted with the clinical term "cure". Recovery is, largely, a grass roots term. In clinical terms, long term abstinence is called "remission". In grass roots venues, there is a cultural application of the word "sober". A recovering addict might refer to recovery as being "clean" and an alcoholic might self-identify as "sober". For some, the term is "clean and sober". In a discussion about that nebulous term "recovery" the distinction between the terms is relevant. In AA, one might observe a person who has been abstinent from alcohol for a considerable time, but still acts in a manner which might be called "dry". A familiar saying in some grass roots cultures is "You can't operate sober the way you did when you were drinking". The cultural perspective of many grass roots recovery venues is that the process of recovery changes the person.

Let's look back at the consequences or characteristics of addiction. There are social consequences which result in social isolation. Early in recovery, many self-identify as isolated or lonely. We further observe that mood and mind altering substances are self-destructive methods of managing moods. That is, social isolation and stress are factors which are correlated with relapse. In layman terms, if one continues to behave in an angry, judgmental, or otherwise anti-social manner, it might result in loss of a job, end of a marriage, or other absence of social support. Therefore, if one does not gain the ability, in recovery, to heal current relationships, and to cultivate productive relationships in the future, the social stress of isolation might return and trigger a return to substance abuse, or "relapse".

We might note the AA (2001) statements: "Selfishness-self-centeredness! That, we think is the root of our troubles. Driven by a hundred forms of fear, self-delusion, self-seeking, and self-pity, we step on the toes of our fellows and they retaliate" (p. 62); "Our liquor was but a symptom" (p. 64).

That is the negative side of the motivation for the lifelong process which we call "recovery". A caution here is the observation that AA (2001) was, essentially written by men. For many women in recovery, or other survivors of trauma, substance abuse or dependency comes from a self-image which is not a result of their own behavior, but is imposed by life circumstance. For these people, there is a later AA publication which moderates the self-criticism of these passages. "At this stage of the inventory proceedings, our sponsors come to the rescue.

They comfort the melancholy one by first showing him that his case is not strange or different…" (AA, 1953, p. 46).

Therefore, we have identified the need for a long term sustained program of recovery. But is there not a positive side to this idea? The bad news is that some people require a lifelong process of recovery to maintain abstinence. The good news is that this process is, essentially, identical to the progression towards "self-actualization." (Maslow, 1943; Rogers, 1961). The suggestion of working with others and being of service to a program, church, or our community is consistent with Christianity and Buddhism. This idea that people in recovery are "pilgrims" on the path to self-actualization, enlightenment, or happiness is suggested by a portion of AA (1976) which appears at the end of the instructive text but before the personal stories, to wit: "We shall be with you in the Fellowship of the Spirit, and you will surely meet some of us as you trudge the Road of Happy Destiny." (p. 164)

Recovery—Spiritual/Moral

We might observe that the word "spirituality" refers to that aspect of the human experience which is mystical, or defies logic, or is so intangible as to defy explanation. In the context of addiction and recovery, however, observations about spirituality and religion seem to be essential. Miller (2010) devotes an entire chapter to "Incorporating spirituality into addiction counseling" (p. 329)

AA (2001) cites Silkworth (1939) as stating: "…unless this person can experience an entire psychic change there is very little hope of his recovery." (p. xxix). In the same volume: "The term 'spiritual experience' and 'spiritual awakening' … shows that the personality change sufficient to bring about recovery from alcoholism…' (p. 567).

One with experience in contemporary management theory might identify this as a "paradigm shift". An addiction counseling professional might say that this shift is necessary to break the barrier of denial. For the professional psychologist, the stages of moral development as defined by Kohlberg and summarized in Kohlberg & Hersh (1977) can be used to identify the relationship between low self-esteem, self-injurious behaviors and the lack of moral maturity. Kohlberg, briefly, identifies the moral development of a child from pre-conventional morality. Doing what is necessary to get what one wants, and avoid punishment. Conventional Morality is the second step where one recognizes the rules of society, family or other environment, and develops the ability to negotiate moral codes of conduct. The final stage, or post-conventional is that state of mind where the individual has developed a moral code of conduct which transcends mere law. This moral code of conduct could be argued to be an element of self-esteem. Therefore, the development of a moral code of conduct in accordance with the definitions by Kohlberg can be identified as an element to the recovery process from a moral and spiritual perspective.

We must note that the distinction between spirituality and religion is important to the recovery process. Briefly, our loose overview is that spirituality is an acceptance of our own limited knowledge and a search for truth and our own moral code. Religion is the acceptance of the spiritual ideas of others and the adoption of a prescribed moral code. We might suggest and observe that each person possesses aspects of both.

We might also observe that a concept of God or dogmatic rules of behavior are resisted more by the addict than the more mainstream personality. This might be a result of the personal isolation, a perception that life itself is dangerous, or excessively painful, or that neither people, nor God can be trusted.

For whatever the reason, however, this spiritual experience appears to be essential to recovery, and has been shown to be important to the process of personal growth and self-actualization. Our discussion here will strive to remove some of the mystery. If we understand better how any process works, it increases our ability to use that process to our own benefit. Notably, this dialogue will attempt to avoid interference with any particular religion or belief system.

Prayer

One could argue for or against the power of prayer on many levels. What we do know is that prayer is of benefit to the people who pray, and the people who think that others are praying for them. Psychology would suggest that this practice has a placebo effect which increases self-efficacy. How prayer is of benefit is less important than the idea that it is effective.

Belief in God

It is interesting to observe that Eurocentric Christianity sees God as a man. Pre-Columbian art in the Americas had a sculpture of a female deity. For a person who has experienced the early loss of a parent, was abused or abandoned by a parent, the understanding that there is an entity which created them might serve to increase the sense of self-worth. It is interesting to note that the idea of a divine conscience, a source of all things is logical in itself, by all standards of thinking. Therefore, the low concept of self, in this context, is illogical.

The caution here might observe that religion has been used for political purposes. It is clear that the social structure of a church serves to marshal resources to carry out the ministry of service to its parishioners and those less fortunate, who they might serve in observation of their faith.

While social structure and power is deemed necessary to the work of the church, this power can be corrupted politically. Religious power can be corrupted and put to use for social oppression, Inquisition, Crusades, and Jihad.

This propensity for the abuse of religious power has been observed and resisted in the United States by the separation of Church and State as provided for in our laws. In grass roots recovery, the "12 Traditions" (AA, 1953) guard against this abuse of social power on many fronts.

For the individual in recovery, for the pilgrim on the path of self-discovery, and for the neophyte to religion, there is a similar danger.

We might suggest that every person has a moral code or a conscience. The paradigm shift in which one comes to realize that they are not all powerful might cause them to observe this innate personal moral code, or a moral code as prescribed by one religion or another. The danger is that a belief in an intervening deity or God can be interpreted selfishly on a personal level in a similar quest for social power or prestige.

There are those who would profess that the creator of the universe intervened on their behalf so when they get probation for felony DUI. This logical process then suggests that God will get them a job. While everyone is entitled to their beliefs, such a self-concept that one is superior because of their faith is the same as the political idea that we should rule or have the right to oppress others because God has so ordained us.

In recovery, this concept of an intervening deity suggests that the little girl who was sexually abused by her uncle is not a child of God. It reinforces the mistaken impression that, somehow, she is bad or of reduced personal value as evidenced by her abandonment by God.

We might suggest here that:

1) Most people have a conscience and an intuitive idea of what is right and wrong for them.

2) People have a tendency to manifest in their lives that which they deserve, based upon their concept of their value as a person.

3) Good works and service to others manifests a self-concept of personal value.

Therefore, it is suggested here that a belief in a Higher Power is the pathway to the acceptance of a higher order of life and an exploration of our place in that order. For many of us, it is the first step in the discovery of who we are and why we are here. (Self-actualization).

For the recovering person, I might suggest that our relationship with our Higher Power should ask a question similar to that offered by JFK (1961) "… ask not what your country can do for you; ask what you can do for your country" (p.145).

This embodies the attitude and the benefit in the belief that there is a Higher Power. In whatever manner one perceives or conceives of a higher authority, there is a self-concept which, on the one hand feels different and isolated. On the other hand is recovery where one feels connected, and if one is really fortunate, perceives themselves as an essential element to their community, their family and even, perhaps, the universe itself.

Therefore, we suggest that the pathways to this self-actualization, this Nirvana, this Enlightenment, this state of loving unity with the Whole begins with an acceptance of the existence of this Whole itself. Whether one perceives God as a man, a woman, or some intangible other: "That which has always been and shall always be. From which all things have come and to which all things shall return. Who is in all things, and knows all things."

Ask not what God can do for you. Ask, rather what you can do to serve God. I cannot risk offending any reader by attempting a list of the prophets, teachers, or others who would agree with this idea.

I can, however, assert with some level of confidence, that this idea will assist you in your attempts at recovery and your search for a sense of belonging and purpose in your life.

If the reader is unsure how this begins, AA (2010), which remains essentially unchanged since its first publication in 1939 offers the third step prayer:

> "God, I offer myself to thee – to build with me and do with me as thou wilt. Relieve me of the bondage of self, that I may better do thy will. Take away my difficulties that victory over them will bear witness to those I would help of thy love, thy power, and thy way of life. May I do thy will always!" (p. 63)

For those of you who are already pilgrims, I offer this work in love and service. Namaste'

References

Alcoholics Anonymous (1953) *Twelve steps and twelve traditions* New York: Alcoholics Anonymous World Services, Inc.

Alcoholics Anonymous (2001) *Alcoholics anonymous* (4th ed.) New York: Alcoholics Anonymous World Services, Inc.

American Psychiatric Association. (2000). *Diagnostic and statistical manual of mental disorders* (3rd ed., rev.). Washington, DC: Author.

Armstrong, Tonya D., and E. Jane Costello. 2002. "Community studies on adolescent substance use, abuse, or dependence and psychiatric comorbidity." *Journal Of Consulting And Clinical Psychology* 70, no. 6: 1224-1239. *PsycARTICLES*, EBSCO*host* (accessed March 26, 2012).

Asbury, W., Ketcham, K., Schulstad, M. & Ciaramicoli, A.(2000) *Beyond the Influence: understanding and defeating alcoholism*. New York: Bantam Books

Baler, R. D., & Volkow, N. D. (2011). Addition as a systems failure: Focus on adolescence and smoking. *Journal Of The American Academy Of Child & Adolescent Psychiatry*, 50(4), 329-339. doi:10.1016/j.jaac.2010.12.008

Bandura, A. (2001) Social cognitive theory: An agentic perspective. *Annual Review of Psychology*. 2001. 52:1-26

Beers, M., Porter, R., Jones, T., Kaplan, J., & Berkwitz (2006) *The Merck manual of diagnosis and therapy*. Whitehouse Station, NY: Merck Research Laboratories.

BJS (2011) *Drugs and crime facts* (website). Washington DC: Bureau of Justice Statistics. Retrieved 12/21/2011 from: http://bjs.ojp.usdoj.gov/content/dcf/duc.cfm

Bolland, J. M., Bryant, C. M., Lian, B. E., McCallum, D. M., Vazsonyi, A. T., & Barth, J. M. (2007). Development and Risk Behavior Among African American, Caucasian, and Mixed-race Adolescents Living in High Poverty Inner-city Neighborhoods. *American Journal Of Community Psychology*, 40(3/4), 230-249. doi:10.1007/s10464-007-9132-1

Bronfenbrenner, U., & Evans, G. W. (2000). Developmental Science in the 21 [sup st] Century: Emerging Questions, Theoretical Models, Research Designs and Empirical Findings. *Social Development*, 9(1), 115-125.

Bronfenbrenner, U. (1986). Ecology of the family as a context for human development: research perspectives. *Developmental Psychology, 22*(6), 723-741.

Bruner & Anglin (1973) *Beyond the information given: studies in the psychology of knowing.* New York: W. W. Norton & Co.

Connors, M. E. (2011). Attachment theory: A "secure base" for psychotherapy integration. *Journal Of Psychotherapy Integration, 21*(3), 348-362. doi:10.1037/a0025460

Darwin, C. (1859) *On the origin of species by means of natural selection.* London: J. Murray.

Durant, W. (1939). *The Life of Greece.* New York, NY : Simon and Schuster.

DOHHS (1990). *Drug and Violence: Causes, Correlates, and Consequences.* Rockville, MD: National Institute on Drug Abuse. Retrieved from: http://www.eric.ed.gov/PDFS/ED341000.pdf

Fitzpatrick, M., Carr, A., Dooley, B., Flanagan-Howard, R., Flanagan, E., Tierney, K., & ... Egan, J. (2010). Profiles of adult survivors of severe sexual, physical and emotional institutional abuse in Ireland. *Child Abuse Review, 19*(6), 387-404.

Freud, S. (1893) The aetiology of the neuroses (Gay, P. ed., 1989) *The Freud Reader.* New York: W. W. Norton & Co.

Harlow, H. F., Dodswoorth, R. O. & Harlow, M. K. (1965) *Total social isolation in monkeys.* University of Wisconsin. Dept. of Psychology Primate Laboratory and Regional Primate Research Center.

Inaba, D., & Cohen, W. (2004) *Uppers, downers, all arounders* (5th ed.) Medford, OR: CNS Productions, Inc.

Johnston, L. D., O'Malley, P. M., Bachman, J. G., & Schulenberg, J. E. (2010). *Monitoring the Future national survey results on drug use, 1975-2009. Volume I: Secondary school students* (NIH Publication No. 10-7584). Bethesda, MD: National Institute on Drug Abuse, 734 pp.

Kelly, J. F., Finney, J. W., & Moos, R. (2004) Substance use disorder patients who are mandated to treatment: characteristics, treatment process, and 1- and 5- year outcomes. *Journal of Substance Abuse Treatment* 28 (2005) 213-223, doi:10.1016/j.jsat.2004.10.014

Kennedy, J. F. (1961) *Inaugural address.* Washington DC; as cited in *Speeches that changed the World .*(2006) (3rd ed.)London: Quercus Publishing, Ltd.

Ketcham, K. & Mueller, A. (1986) *Eating right to live sober.* New York: Signet Books

Kohlberg, L., & Hersh, R. (1977). Moral development: A review of the theory. *Theory Into Practice, 16*(2), 53-59. doi:10.1080/00405847709542675.

Lee, S., Lyvers, M., & Edwards, M. (2008). Childhood sexual abuse and substance abuse in relation to depression and coping. *Journal of Substance Use,* 13(5), 346-360. doi:10.1080/14659890802211077

Maslow, A. H. (1943) *Hierarchy of needs: A theory of human motivation.* (Kindle Version) www.all-about-psychology.com

Miller, G. (2010) *Learning the language of addiction counseling.* (3rd ed.) Hoboken, NJ: John Wiley and Sons

Mishne, J. (1984). Trauma of parent loss through divorce, death, and illness. *Child & Adolescent Social Work Journal,* 1(2), 74-88. doi:10.1007/BF00757387.

Nardi, D. A., & Delunas, L. (2000). Development, preliminary testing and use of the Parenting Tracking Form in perinatal addiction treatment. *Addiction Research,* 8(4), 399-412. doi:10.3109/16066350009009523

Piaget, J. & Inhelder, B. (1969) *The psychology of the child.* (Weaver, H. trans.) New York: Harper Collins

Roberts, A. C., Nishimoto, R. H., & Kirk, R. S. (2003). Cocaine abusing women who report sexual abuse: Implications for treatment. *Journal Of Social Work Practice In The Addictions,* 3(1), 5-24. doi:10.1300/J160v03n01_02

Rogers, C. (1961). *On becoming a person: A therapist's view of psychotherapy*: Boston: Houghton Mifflin

Sagan, C. & Druyan, A. (1992) *Shadows of forgotten ancestors: a search for who we are.* New York: Random House

Silkworth, R, MD (1939) *The doctor's opinion* (as cited in AA, 2001) New York: Alcoholics Anonymous World Services.

Stroop, J. R. (1935). Studies of interference in serial verbal reactions. *Journal of Experimental Psychology,* 18, 643-662

Sullivan, P. F. (1995) Mortality in anorexia nervosa. *American Journal of Psychiatry* Am J Psychiatry. 1995 Jul;152(7):1073-4. Retrieved May 7, 2012 from: http://www.ncbi.nlm.nih.gov/pubmed/7793446

Tennant, C., & Bernardi, E. (1988). Childhood loss in alcoholics and narcotic addicts. *British Journal Of Addiction,* 83(6), 695-703. doi:10.1111/j.1360-0443.1988.tb02600.x

Thurman, S., & Berry, B. E. (1992). Cocaine use: Implications for intervention with childbearing women and their infants. *Children's Health Care,* 21(1), 31-38. doi:10.1207/s15326888chc2101_5Tinbergen, N. (1965) *Animal Behavior.* New York: Time Incorporated

Wadsworth, M. E., Raviv, T., Reinhard, C., Wolff, B., Santiago, C., & Einhorn, L. (2008). An Indirect Effects Model of the Association Between Poverty and Child Functioning: The Role of Children's Poverty-Related Stress. *Journal Of Loss & Trauma,* 13(2/3), 156-185. doi:10.1080/15325020701742185

Wright, R. (1994) *The moral animal: why we are the way we are: the new science of evolutionary psychology*. New York: Pantheon Books.

Yates, T. (2009). Developmental pathways from child maltreatment to nonsuicidal self-injury. *Understanding nonsuicidal self-injury: Origins, assessment, and treatment* (pp. 117-137). Washington, DC US: American Psychological Asssociation